WINE MEMORIES

MIS EN BOUTEILLES AU CHATEAU

CHATEAU LAFITE
1943
Bᵒⁿˢde ROTHSCHILD, Propriétaires

BORDEAUX   FRANCE

DÉPOSÉ

WINE MEMORIES

GREAT WRITERS ON THE PLEASURES OF WINE

Edited by Sara Nicklès
Introduction by Brian St. Pierre

CHRONICLE BOOKS
SAN FRANCISCO

Pages 140–142 constitute a continuation of the copyright page.

*Every effort has been made to trace the ownership of all copyrighted material
included in this volume. Any errors that may have occurred are inadvertent
and will be corrected in subsequent editions, provided notification is sent to
the publisher.*

*To maintain the authentic style of each writer included herein, quirks of
spelling and grammar remain unchanged from their original state.*

Library of Congress Cataloging-in-Publication Data available.

ISBN 0-8118-2645-7

Printed in Hong Kong.
Design: Sara Schneider
Cover photograph: Deborah Jones

Distributed in Canada by Raincoast Books
8680 Cambie Street
Vancouver, British Columbia V6P 6M9

10 9 8 7 6 5 4 3 2 1

Chronicle Books
85 Second Street
San Francisco, California 94105

www.chroniclebooks.com

CONTENTS

All wines are by their very nature full of reminiscence, the golden tears and red blood summers that are gone.

—RICHARD LE GALLIENNE

A bottle of good wine, like a good act, shines ever in the retrospect.

—ROBERT LOUIS STEVENSON

1994

NAPA VALLEY

CABERNET SAUVIGNON

RESERVE

UNFILTERED

ROBERT MONDAVI WINERY

ALCOHOL 13.5% BY VOLUME

"WE'LL ALWAYS HAVE PARIS," HUMPHREY BOGART SAYS TO INGRID Bergman at the end of *Casablanca*, and we know just what he means: The really good memories are imperishable. I've also come to realize that often those memories involve wine, in one way or another. (It was champagne for Rick and Ilsa in the movie.)

One of my best memories is the time I discovered Burgundy. I started at the top, which was a 1959 La Tâche, one of the best vintages ever of one of the best wines in the world, from the Domaine de la Romanée-Conti. My regular house wine at the time (1966) was a California red that didn't require a corkscrew, so you can probably imagine the jump I was taking when I had my first glass. (I also learned, incidentally, that good wine memories aren't made by sips at tastings, but by drinks, where your senses have room to stretch and move around.)

I had to hunt all over Manhattan and Brooklyn and northern New Jersey for more of that wine (La Tâche means "the task," which seemed only too appropriate after a while). I finally found two bottles. Then came the dilemma all wine-lovers face with gorgeous rarities—good wine needs to be shared, but when there isn't going to be any more, generosity must be tempered with enlightened self-interest. The love of my life at the time was the obvious beneficiary, not only for romantic reasons but also because she didn't drink very much, and I built a dinner around the wine. I still remember everything about the occasion and the bottomless flavor of that ruby-red liquid, which is fortunate, because a few months later when the lady decided to become my ex, she took the other bottle and I've never seen another one since. So: Bless the memory; it's as lovely now as the day it was born.

I had no words for wine then, and self-consciously shied away from a lot of what was being written about it, until I read a description of a fine Burgundy as an iron fist in a velvet glove, and realized I knew what the writer meant. Then, I went on a European literary binge and found an abundance of great writing, so much of it involving wine: there were rivers of it in Hemingway, lyrical streams in Colette, it was fuel for Henry Miller's nocturnal ramblings, inspiration for the heroic gastronomic musings of A. J. Leibling (who wrote often of Paris). Back home, the Beat Generation was lubricated by cheap red wine, which was all that writers could afford when we were getting ten cents a word and publishers were turning down long poems and essays. It made for powerful memories, too; mostly of awful mornings trying to get over it.

We moved on, and so did wine. That '59 La Tâche has probably been surpassed several times in the last four decades, and it has more company in the rarified air of greatness than ever before. That's just as well. As Frank Prial notes in the anthology that follows, the game of naming your "best bottle" can get deliciously complicated after a while, especially when time and place and mood and friends—and then food—all conspire with wine to get your vote for the top spot. It's fortunate that the memory box is expandable, because there's always more to fill it with. Here are many memories on the varietal pleasures of wine. ♀

1923

Grand Vin

CHATEAU DE MYRAT

BARSAC

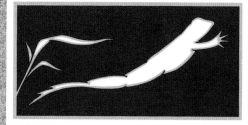

FROG'S LEAP

1998 SAUVIGNON BLANC
NAPA VALLEY

PRODUCED & BOTTLED BY FROG'S LEAP, RUTHERFORD, CA

ALC. 13.5% BY VOL.

RED WINE

TOM McNAMEE

THIS WAS THE SUMMER, BETWEEN MY FRESHMAN AND SOPHO-more years in college, when I fell in love with Louise Rossett. I wanted to take her to Justine's, the fanciest restaurant in Memphis, and I wanted to have wine. In those days, you had to bring your own. I was underage, but my research had identified a liquor store that would sell wine to minors—only wine, and only if you acted serious. I asked the man to suggest a wine to take to Justine's, which was so grand it had no sign out front. He asked what we were going to eat and how much I wanted to spend. I said I was probably going to have the famous crabmeat Justine—no, the tournedos, he countered—and could spend five dollars. "If you're willing to go to eight," he said, "I'll give you something you'll never forget." I was in love, so I splurged.

The maître d'hôtel scowled at the label, raised his eyebrows, and murmured something to a waiter. Justine's policy was to stick teenagers in a back room, but we were marched in state to the front parlor. The waiter replaced the regular glasses with giant, glittering globes. When he poured me a taste of my wine, and its dark, sweet, soul-deep scent billowed into the room, I knew that this was not like screwtop Lake Country Red, the only other wine I'd ever tasted. And oh, my. I had not known till this moment that anything could taste this good. I studied the label, telling myself to remember it. It was Château Lafite-Rothschild of the 1961 vintage. Eight bucks. I resolved then and there I would marry Louise. ♀

GRAND VIN DE BEAUNE GRÈVES

APPELLATION BEAUNE PREMIER CRU CONTRÔLÉE

VIGNE DE L'ENFANT JÉSUS

1996

ESTATE GROWN, PRODUCED AND BOTTLED BY

BOUCHARD PÈRE & FILS

CHÂTEAU DE BEAUNE, CÔTE D'OR, FRANCE

ALC. 13.5% BY VOL.

PRODUIT DE FRANCE · PRODUCT OF FRANCE

750 ML

RED BURGUNDY WINE

BORDEAUX WINEMAKERS HAVE LITTLE USE FOR BURGUNDY vintners, and vice versa. One of my friends was Alexis Lichine, who started out his professional life as a dealer of French wines in the U.S., wrote many wonderful books about wine, and was a romantic figure with all sorts of ladies. Eventually, he bought a vineyard of his own—the Château Prieuré-Lichine and Lascombes, where he bottled several respectable wines.

I was his guest, and Alexis, who knew all the great growers in Bordeaux, took me on a tour of their chateaux and caves.

Lichine gave me a short course in the economics of wine. "When it's a poor year for wine, caused by severe weather, the price goes up, because there is a shortage of drinkable vintage. When it's a great weather year, and there is an abundance of grapes and all the elements are in our favor, the price also goes up."

"Why is that?"

"Because everybody fights to buy a good year."

Lichine briefed me on wine-tasting in his own cellars. "Always swish the wine around in your mouth clockwise for Bordeaux, counter-clockwise for Burgundy. Never swallow it; spit it out."

We went to the Château Margaux and the Château Latour, and I spat. Lichine was pleased with his pupil. Our last stop was Château Mouton-Rothschild, owned by Philippe de Rothschild. Mr. Rothschild, a charming host, showed us through his caves and then invited us to an elegantly furnished glass salon overlooking all his vineyards. One of the many priceless items in the room was an eighteenth-century rug. A servant came by and handed me a glass of champagne. I swished it around in my mouth. Lichine looked at me in horror, and screamed, "NO!"

It was too late. I spat it on the carpet.

Years later, my article about spitting on his rug appeared in the French *Reader's Digest.* Rothschild was so impressed he had a case of Mouton Rothschild 1959 delivered to my house in Washington. I put it in my cellar. No one who came to my home was worthy of a bottle.

At the time, the Vietnam war was raging in earnest, and my children and their friends cared little for anything. One day, I was up in the attic and I saw in the corner a pile of empty wine bottles. In disbelief, I realized they had once contained my Rothschild wine. I let out a blood-curdling scream, went downstairs, and confronted my daughter. "Why did you take my French wine from the cellar?" I demanded.

She said, "We couldn't find any Blue Nun." ♀

Gutsabfüllung
Weingut

von Hövel

Oberemmel/Saar
Deutschland
Produce of Germany

Qualitätswein
mit Prädikat

750 ml e

ALC.8.5 % BY Vol.
A.P.Nr.3 525 781-5-98

MOSEL-SAAR-RUWER

von Hövel

1997 er
Oberemmeler Hütte
Riesling Kabinett

THE SUN ALSO RISES
ERNEST HEMINGWAY

"NOW," THE COUNT BROUGHT UP A BOTTLE. "I THINK THIS IS COOL."

I brought a towel and he wiped the bottle dry and held it up. "I like to drink champagne from magnums. The wine is better but it would have been too hard to cool." He held the bottle, looking at it. I put out the glasses.

"I say. You might open it," Brett suggested.

"Yes, my dear. Now I'll open it."

It was amazing champagne.

"I say that is wine," Brett held up her glass. "We ought to toast something. 'Here's to royalty.'"

"This wine is too good for toast-drinking, my dear. You don't want to mix emotions up with a wine like that. You lose the taste."

Brett's glass was empty.

"You ought to write a book on wines, count," I said.

"Mr. Barnes," answered the count, "all I want out of wines is to enjoy them." ♈

GABBIANO

Chianti

DENOMINAZIONE DI ORIGINE
CONTROLLATA
E GARANTITA

1990

PRODUCED AND BOTTLED BY C.S.C. - TAVARNELLE V.P. (FI) FOR ICARO S.P.A.
750 ML   PRODUCT OF ITALY   ALC.12% BY VOL.

CATENA

ALTA

1996
MALBEC
LUNLUNTA

MENDOZA · ARGENTINA

Alc. by vol. 13.7°/₀

THE BEST BOTTLE

FRANK J. PRIAL

WHEN THE TALK TURNS TO WINE, I CAN USUALLY HOLD MY own. But there is one game of wine one-upmanship that is always difficult to play: that business about the best bottle.

It starts off innocently enough with a story about a trip or a dinner. "They served us the 1955 so-and-so and, really, it was the best bottle of wine I've ever had."

Someone else picks it up. "Oh, the '55? We had the '29 in Paris last year." And so it goes. Eventually, it's my turn. "I'll bet you've had some fantastic wines," someone prompts.

True. But which was the best? There have been some extraordinary wines. There was the 1870 Château Mouton Rothschild at a dinner in Mouton just last October—and there was the 1916 that preceded it and the 1921 Château d'Yquem that followed it, all at the same meal.

There were, a couple of years ago an Ay, in the Champagne region, two bottles of the 1914 Bollinger. They had a slight patina of age and an unforgettable mellowness, but were as fresh and lively as a 1970 bottle.

There was a 1943 Musigny, made from pre-*phylloxera* vines. There was that 1958 Cabernet Sauvignon in San Francisco a year or two back and the extraordinary 1935 Simi Zinfandel we had at the winery in Healdsburg just a few months ago.

Should I—could I—pick one of these as the best? It would mean leaving out a couple of memorable Trockenbeerenauslese, the rarest of all German wines, including a 1959 from the Bernkasteler Doktor Vineyard, opened in the cellars of Karl Lauerburg, one of the vineyard owners, in fall, 1976.

It would mean, too, omitting a superb 1945 Château Haut-Brion savored in Bordeaux five years ago, and it would require ignoring a great panoply of younger but already magnificent wines—such as a Bonnes-Mares from the vineyard of Comte de Vogüe or a Chambolle-Musigny, Les Charmes, from the Grivelet vineyard, both wines from the 1966 vintage.

The easiest way out, of course, would be to pick one of these wines—any one—build it up a bit, say it was undoubtedly the greatest and let it go at that. But it wouldn't be the truth. The correct answer should be: none of the above.

Wine drinking is not a sterile, academic business of vineyard's names and vintages and esoteric trappings: proper glasses, optimum temperatures, and all that. Any professional can recall wines that showed poorly in tastings only to come into their own, with great style, at the lunch or dinner that followed the serious sniffing and sipping.

Caught up in a game of "best bottle," how could I admit that one of the most memorable of all for me was a jug of Almadén Mountain Chablis shared one warm Sunday afternoon, in 1954, with four other sailors on the Coast Guard cutter *McLane.*

We had come in from a wearing, pounding patrol and were tied up at our regular berth at Aberdeen, Washington on the coast southwest of Seattle. Most of the crew was on liberty but the cook had prepared a lovely batch of fried rabbit for those of us still on board.

It was our first decent meal in days. Not having the ship bucking under us was a treat in itself, but the combination of the warm spring breeze, the view of the river and the fir forests beyond, the rabbit, and that cold wine made for an afternoon few gourmet chefs could surpass.

The fact that the jug was illegal probably made the meal even more interesting. But we were in port and there was no one around. . . .

There is a bottle of wine that, with luck, I get to sample every year or so and, each time I do, I swear it is the pinnacle of the winemaking art. It isn't, of course, but don't argue. It is that bottle of the house Sancerre that begins every meal I enjoy at Chez Allard, still one of the all-time great bistros of Paris.

I have no idea where Allard gets his Sancerre. The label says simply that the wine is bottled for Allard, 41 rue St. André des Arts, and that it is of a very recent vintage.

Is it the best of all Sancerres? Would it triumph in a blind tasting, with all those white coats and clipboards and spittoons for the judges? Who knows? Who cares? It's a well-made wine. It is served young and fresh and cold and it is used to wash down some of the finest seafood in Paris in one of the friendliest restaurants in the world.

Of the famous bottles I mentioned, that 1943 Musigny stands out. So do the two 1914 Bollingers. The Musigny was a gift from Roger Chauveron when he closed up the Café Chauveron on East 53rd Street. Drinking it a year or so later it brought back memories of magical dinners at the Chauveron at its peak as well as long afternoons spent in the deserted restaurant listening to Chauveron tell stories about the restaurant business in Paris in his boyhood, only a few of which ever found their way into the profile of him I later wrote.

The Bollinger? It was great Champagne, of course. But who could sip it looking out over the rolling vineyards leading down to the Marne without thinking of that fateful year in which it was made—1914? That's the sort of thing that makes a bottle memorable.

That 1966 Bonnes-Mares was excellent, but I remember even more a tasting of Bonnes-Mares in Nuits-St.-Georges in December, 1975. I had driven down from Paris to spend a week in the Beaujolais country. I was irritated because the schedule left no time before leaving Paris to see a three-gallery show of pictures by an artist I greatly admire, Bernard Cathelin.

Driving back north, I had a choice of bypassing Burgundy and going straight through to Paris to see the Cathelin show, or of stopping off in Burgundy to visit Jacques Seysses, the young genius whose Domaine Dujac I knew was producing some of the finest wines in Burgundy.

I chose the Domaine Dujac and called Jacques from Villefranche. He promised to set up an interesting tasting. After searching in a cold, driving rain, I located the Seysses' home, upstairs over an old cellar in the center of Nuits-St.-Georges. To my astonishment, I found myself being welcomed into a magnificent modern home, where I was completely surrounded by paintings by Bernard Cathelin. "Oh," said Mr. Seysses, "but he was the best man at our wedding."

We tasted every Domaine Dujac Bonnes-Mares since the first in 1969. They are extremely fine wines but to drink them among the Cathelins made them even more extraordinary for me.

The finest bottle? Perhaps it was a huge *fiasco* of Chianti we had one day in a vast *trattoria* in Florence. It had been a long trip; there had been a number of dinners in private homes and in elegant restaurants. But nothing could compare with the bustle, the noise, the friendliness of that *trattoria*. The jug of wine came without having been requested. It was placed in the center of the table already one-third empty. As we ate, we drank. When the meal was over, the waiter squinted at the bottle with a practiced eye and estimated how much we had drunk. It was added to our bill. It came to about $2. Not a great wine, but certainly a memorable bottle.

People often say: "I had this wonderful little wine at an outdoor place in Capri. It was marvelous. But when I finally located a bottle of it here, it tasted awful."

Of course, it could have been poorly handled on the long and bumpy trip from wherever it was made to where it was drunk. Some wines literally do not travel. Memories are different. Every time we look back on a trip to, say, Capri, the sky is brighter, the water bluer, the girls more beautiful, and the wine, well, the wine seems better, too.

Few other things are so dependent on place and time and mood for their impact as wine. Oh, it can be a solitary pleasure. Gulbenkian, the millionaire, once said a perfect dinner required two people: himself and a good maître d'hôtel. I myself recall staying on at a French country house after the crowd had left and eating lunch alone in the 12th century refectory. One day for lunch the house-keeper brought out a 1966 Château Pouget, a fourth growths Margaux, little known in this country. Dining alone at that place at that time, the Pouget seemed without question to be the best bottle of wine in the world.

Once Baron Philippe de Rothschild was asked about the best bottle he ever tasted. "It was a Mouton, of course," he replied. Then, he sat back, smiled, and looked off in the distance. "It was right here in this room," he began. "It was a brilliant evening...." It was ten minutes before he got around to the wine and I forget now what vintage it was. The people and the talk made the wine what it was.

In truth, it really is almost impossible to single out a "best" bottle. But then, it would be wrong to be doctrinaire about the matter—which makes wine such a fascinating interest. That best bottle? Who knows? It may be the one we open tonight. ♇

Bott Frères

VITICULTEURS
VINS D'ALSACE
RIBEAUVILLÉ
(Haut-Rhin)

TOKAY 1921

ON CLARET

JOHN KEATS

I NEVER DRINK ABOVE THREE GLASSES OF WINE, AND NEVER any spirits and water; though, by the bye, the other day Woodhouse took me to his coffee-house, and ordered a bottle of claret. How I like claret! When I can get claret, I must drink it. 'Tis the only palate affair that I am at all sensual in. Would it not be a good spec. to send you some vine-roots? Could it be done? I'll inquire. If you could make some wine like claret, to drink on summer evenings in an arbor! It fills one's mouth with a gushing freshness, then goes down cool and feverless: then, you do not feel it quarreling with one's liver. No; 'tis rather a peacemaker and lies as quiet as it did in the grape. Then it is as fragrant as the Queen Bee, and the more ethereal part mounts into the brain, not assaulting the cerebral apartments, like a bully looking for his trull, and hurrying from door to door, bouncing against the wainscot, but rather walks like Aladdin about his enchanted palace, so gently that you do not feel his step. Other wines of a heavy and spirituous nature transform a man into a Silenus, this makes him a Hermes, and gives a woman the soul and immortality of an Ariadne, for whom Bacchus always kept a good cellar of claret, and even of that he could never persuade her to take above two cups. I said this same claret is the only palate-passion I have; I forgot game; I must plead guilty to the breast of a partridge, the back of a hare, the back-bone of a grouse, the wing and side of a pheasant, and a woodcock *passim*. ♀

CAPE MENTELLE
WESTERN AUSTRALIA

SHIRAZ 1997
MARGARET RIVER

ALCOHOL 14.5% BY VOLUME
PRODUCT OF AUSTRALIA

MONSIEUR DE MONTILLE SWIRLED THE WINE AND WATCHED how it moved. He held it up to the light. He stuck his generous nose into the glass and inhaled the fragrance. He took a sip. He considered. A solid man with a smooth, bald pate and the shrewd look of the lawyer that he was, he threw back his head as he tasted the wine, letting it linger in his throat. From the walls of his dining room, which looked as if it had not changed in centuries, his ancestors looked indulgently down.

"There is sunlight in the glass," he said finally, "much sunlight. It is from a very good year." He took another sip, nodded, turned to his wife. They conferred. Not a '69, surely, it was not that old. A '71 then, they were agreed. "Such glycerine," said Monsieur, "what can it be?"

When Kermit told him what it was de Montille cried, "But I have this wine in my cellar!" He turned eagerly to Kermit and asked, "Did Ampeau sell to you?"

Kermit nodded smugly.

"Consider yourself honored," he said, "and don't count on it happening again. He has whims."

Kermit looked glum.

"Don't take it personally," put in Madame de Montille gently. "He is the strangest man. They say that even when he goes to mass he runs in putting on his clothes. And as he leaves the church he is already undressing so as not to lose time. He is devoted to the vines."

Kermit was eager to get down to business, but in Burgundy the meal always comes first. This one had been created to show off the wines. It began unexceptionally with a modest Passetoutgrains and a salad laced with herbs and rich with garlic.

Then there was civet de lièvre. "The specialty of the region," said Madame proudly as her husband went around the table pouring out a '64 Rugiens. He sipped the wine and nodded with satisfaction.

The less hardy '66 Rugiens was served with cheese made by the neighbors. And then, finally, Monsieur de Montille brought out a mold-encrusted bottle of '57 Volnay to serve with the tarte aux pommes. I took a sip and it danced in my mouth. It was alive with flavor, like no wine I had ever tasted. I looked around to see if everyone liked it as much as I did. Monsieur de Montille looked happy; even Kermit looked impressed. Then Monsieur de Montille took a second sip and his smile faded. "Too bad," he said softly.

I took another sip. The dance had stopped. *"C'est mort,"* said Monsieur de Montille with finality.

Lunch over, we descended into the cellar. It was a low-ceilinged room filled with casks; the bare bulbs cast a dim golden light. We tasted the Passetoutgrains, the Volnay, the simple burgundies. Monsieur de Montille shook his head. "We made a mistake this year," he said sadly. "We made too much. It was a very big harvest. The wine is fine, it will be very correct, very *comme il faut,* but . . ." As we moved to the '78s he nodded appreciatively and said, almost to himself, "This is a wine with character. The '79s will never be like the '78s." ♀

JEAN MORIN *PROPRIÉTAIRE*
du Château de la Tour au Clos-Vougeot

CHATEAU DE LA TOUR

CLOS·VOUGEOT

APPELLATION CLOS-VOUGEOT CONTROLÉE

CHAMPAGNE

TRUMAN CAPOTE

EVEN FOR THOSE WHO DISLIKE CHAMPAGNE . . . THERE ARE two Champagnes one can't refuse: Dom Perignon and the even superior Cristal, which is bottled in a natural-coloured glass that displays its pale blaze, a chilled fire of such prickly dryness that, swallowed, seems not to have been swallowed at all, but instead to have been turned to vapours on the tongue, and burned there to one sweet ash. ♀

1996

LE CIGARE VOLANT

RED WINE

CALIFORNIA

ALCOHOL 13.5% BY VOLUME
PRODUCED AND BOTTLED BY BONNY DOON VINEYARD
SANTA CRUZ, CA • U.S.A. • EARTH

M. F. K. FISHER

WE WENT UP THE WIDE PLEASANT STAIRS TO THE FIRST FLOOR, and into one of the four *chambres bourguignonnes,* in the tumbled process of being turned out between guests. A young Maillard, an attractive solid-looking man who had spent several years in prison camps and confessed that he still ate green salads with a barely repressed gluttony, told us that the rooms were no more in demand than any others in their price range, but that when travelers found that one was available, they would take it with an understandable mixture of amusement and curiosity, in spite of the noise from the street and the station.

We went through a large simple bedroom hung with soft green, past two beds which were low and "modern" and the two shuttered windows which looked out into trees along the Rue de la Liberté, and into the bathroom. I felt a kind of quiet nervousness in both myself and my companions: was I going to be annoyed, scoffing, repelled, shocked, by this really ridiculous idea of piping good wine through the walls like water?

"And there it is," Georges said without expression. "You will notice that Monsieur Maillard has very prudently placed it near the washbasin, in case some tipsy guest forgets to turn it off properly, and it dribbles."

"More teasing," Maillard said mildly. "Go right ahead, old fellow. You know such a thing has never occurred."

On the wall to the side of the basin, and about breast-high, was what looked like the front half of a fat little wooden wine cask, with two toy spigots sticking out and two pretty little silver *tastevins,* typically Burgundian, hanging beside them. It was the sort of fakey amusing toy an assistant director in Hollywood might order built into his bar, filled with scotch for his housewarming party and then a dust catcher until he became a producer and ordered a bigger and better one. . . .

Monsieur Maillard rather solemnly took down one of the *tastevins* and half filled it with a couple of tablespoons of red wine. "The reservoir is almost empty," he said as he handed it to me. "It is filled every morning, on the top floor, and of course checked at night. In the summer we keep the white wine chilled, but we leave the red alone."

The wine was a good firm *grand ordinaire,* the same Georges and I had drunk downstairs for lunch. It was, the proprietor's son told us, one of the *passe-tous-grains,* a yield from the noble Pinot Noir grape, stretched with Gamay, which some vintners lied about but he felt proud to serve as what it was. Certainly it was pleasant to drink, and he said smilingly that he had never had any complaints about it, either in his restaurant or up in the bedrooms.

I did not taste the white wine, but recognized it from the day before, when I had drunk it at my friend's house with some cold ham and a mild cheese. It had been correctly labeled as an Aligoté, and like the red was a *grand ordinaire* from the southern edge of the Côte d'Or, near Mâcon. By now, in spite of the basically ridiculous position I was in, crowded with two gentlemen in a small bathroom with a fake silver winetaster in my hand, it was plain that I was not at all annoyed, repelled, shocked, or even faintly scoffing. The discreet unvoiced tension vanished. I drained the last sip of the *passe-tous-grains* and as we went out through the shadowy peaceful bedroom I said, "I'm truly glad I saw that, you know."

Georges laughed, and said to Monsieur Maillard, "I showed you the clippings Madame sent. It seems that the venerable wine-and-food boys in the States were really upset at the thought of your vulgar publicity stunt. They envisioned crowds of drunken American tourists, roaring and hiccoughing out of the hotel, spreading scandal and general ill-will."

The young Frenchman grinned comfortably. "I have a pile of clippings a foot high, mostly from America and England! It was indeed a kind of stunt, but I never considered it vulgar. And it has never contributed to the alcoholic problems of the world. The average consumption for two guests in twenty-four hours is much less than a quart, and of course it is mainly white in hot weather and red in the cooler months."

When I asked him which nationality drank the most, he looked thoughtful and said he had not noticed, but would devote himself to some sort of census during the next winter.

. . . Several times over several years I went back to the little bathrooms. It still irked me to tap a cool decent white wine (best before breakfast!) from between the toilet and the washbasin, but I surmounted this aesthetic quibble bravely. And late at night, when traffic thinned below the windows and mysterious bleeps and hummings came from the station, I slipped unsodden into

Burgundian dreams with a *tastevin* of "the red" beside my bed.

I had done my earnest best by letter to reassure Yankee doubters that this was no more a trick than any other. It was as logical as the American pipe dream of constant ice water, once as prerequisite to elegant hotel life as air conditioning seems to be in the seventies. There were other things to worry about, perhaps more politic . . . but not then, in Dijon. ♀

Aus dem Weingute Geh-Rat Dr. v. Basser-mann-Jordan Rheinpfalz Deidesheim

IN VITE VITA

1997 Forster Jesuitengarten
Riesling Kabinett
Pfalz

Qualitätswein mit Prädikat
A.P.Nr. 5 106 064 47 98

750 ml Alc. 10.5% by vol.

Gutsabfüllung
Weingut v. Bassermann-Jordan, D-67142 Deidesheim

PRODUCE OF GERMANY

MY LIFE IN WINE

CALVIN TRILLIN

APRIL 27, 1985

I think it would be fair to say that I was in the Napa Valley recently as a wine consultant. Yes, I'm aware that you didn't realize I know anything about wine. You have been under the impression that when it comes to my feeding habits I might be just a tiny bit unsophisticated. Don't be afraid to say so. I know what you're thinking: You don't understand how someone whose name has any number of times been used in the same sentence with phrases like "pigging out" could be a wine consultant in the Napa Valley. Maybe the reason you don't understand is that you don't know precisely what a wine consultant in the Napa Valley does. After all, you have never been one yourself. I thought I'd just mention that.

Yes, I did rather enjoy eating in the San Francisco Bay Area while I was out there. What was that? Too sophisticated? No, I did not find the New California Cuisine too sophisticated. Yes, I'll admit that I was relieved to find that there were still some pigeons left in the squares of San Francisco; it had occurred to me that since my previous visit, every last one of them might have been snatched up, smoked, and thrown on a bed of radicchio. Yes, it is true that I once expressed some concern about the amount of goat cheese being served in the Bay Area, but that was before I learned that you don't have to kill a goat to get the cheese. I like the New California Cuisine. I like California wine, too. I think it has integrity. Plenty of integrity.

No, this is not some sort of mistake. Yes, I know you had associated me more with soda pop, or maybe beer. Domestic beer. It just goes to show you. People have hidden facets. Here's one of my hidden facets: I don't know much about soda pop. It was only five or six years ago that I acquired (from a San Francisco radio talk-show host named Jim Eason) the basic drill on which soft drink goes with which sort of food. It's Coke or Royal Crown with meat, 7-Up or ginger ale with fish, and Dr. Pepper with game. But you must have known that all along. Even though I didn't, I must say I spent a lot of my childhood eating hamburgers washed down with cherry Cokes—precisely the proper combination. When it comes to connoisseurship, I suppose there must be such a thing as a natural instinct.

Still, I don't make any claims about being an authority on soda pop. My daughter came home from school one day recently with the announcement that Coke and 7-Up were impossible to tell apart if you tasted them while blindfolded and holding your nose. I suppose someone who is sure of his ground on soda pop questions might have said, "Ten bucks says you're wrong, buster," or something like that. I didn't. I was willing to give it a try. What she hadn't said was that it isn't easy to drink Coke or 7-Up while holding your nose, unless you're the sort of person who approaches nose-holding from above. Being blindfolded didn't help either. But I gave it a try, and, as it happens, I was able to tell Coke from 7-Up. I don't claim to know much about soda pop, but aftertaste I know.

I don't know much about beer, either. That's another one of my hidden facets. Yes, I know I've been in any number of late-night conversations with the sort of drinkers whose pedantry about beer increases with their consumption of it. But I don't say much in those conversations. If someone asks me whether I like a particular beer, I say yes. It's true; I like them all. I feel the same way about beer that I feel about ocean views: I'm always happy to have one, but I wouldn't want to put any money on my ability to distinguish among them.

Actually, I don't think many beer pedants can tell one beer from another, any more than those traveling salesmen who think they're impressing the cocktail waitress by saying "J&B on the rocks with a twist" could tell J&B from the sort of Scotch served at faculty cocktail parties. I don't think it would even be necessary to require them to hold their noses during the test, although I'll admit that a roomful of blindfolded traveling salesmen drinking J&B on the rocks while holding their noses might make a pretty sight.

I was asked to be a consultant by my friend Bruce, who makes wine in the Napa Valley. For someone who works in the wine trade, Bruce is quite open-minded. Unlike some other Napa wine people I met on a previous visit, he had not dismissed out of hand my observation, made during a discussion about similarities in certain American and French wines, that both Manischewitz Cream Pink Catawba and Château Lafite-Rothschild taste rather Jewish. Also, he has admitted to me that when blindfolded even wine experts cannot usually tell red wine from white wine. This is astonishing but absolutely true. Check it out. Yes, I do occasionally write something that is absolutely true. It's one of my hidden facets.

During my recent trip to the Napa Valley, Bruce and I met for a drink, and he said he needed some wine advice. I figured Bruce needed the sort of guidance that can sometimes be provided by people who have a natural instinct for connoisseurship—say, whether pinot noir would be appropriate with hog jowls. Yes, if you must know, I was a bit flattered.

What he needed, Bruce said, was some help figuring out how to make his wine attractive to people who know so little about wine that they choose it according to the name or the label design or the price or, in extreme cases, the shape of the bottle. I looked around the bar. We were the only ones there.

"For instance," Bruce said, "what sort of scene do you like on the label?"

I thought it over for a few moments. I finally concluded that what Bruce wanted was, in fact, simply a type of wine consultation. But you must have known that all along.

"A mountain," I said. "I like a nice mountain."

At that moment the waitress showed up to take our order.

"I'll have a glass of red wine," Bruce said. "Unless you feel like bringing white."

"J&B on the rocks for me," I said. "With a twist." ♉

BLANC DE NOIRS

NAPA VALLEY
CHAMPAGNE

VINTAGE 1995

PRODUCED AND BOTTLED BY SCHRAMSBERG VINEYARDS·CALISTOGA CALIFORNIA
ALCOHOL 12% BY VOLUME   CONTENTS 750 MLS

NOTHING APPALLS ME MORE THAN TO HEAR PEOPLE REFER TO the drinking of wine as if it were a forbidden and fascinating way of sneaking alcohol into one's system. My flesh creeps when I hear the legitimate love of the fruit of the vine treated as if it were a longer-winded way of doing what the world does with grain neutral spirits and cheap vermouth. With wine at hand, the good man concerns himself, not with getting drunk, but with *drinking in* all the natural delectabilities of wine: taste, color, bouquet; its manifold graces; the way it complements food and enhances conversation; and its sovereign power to turn evenings into occasions, to lift eating beyond nourishment to conviviality, and to bring the race, for a few hours at least, to that happy state where men are wise and women beautiful, and even one's children begin to look promising. If someone wants the bare effects of alcohol in his bloodstream, let him drink the nasty stuff neat, or have a physician inject it. But do not let him soil my delight with his torpedo-juice mentality. ⧖

1989 **Veuve Clicquot Ponsardin** 1989
par Clicquot Ponsardin
REIMS
FRANCE

LA GRANDE DAME
Champagne

B R U T
à REIMS FRANCE

ÉLABORÉ PAR VEUVE CLICQUOT PONSARDIN REIMS FRANCE NM-157-002

PRODUIT DE FRANCE   PRODUCE OF FRANCE

CHAMPAGNE
APPELLATION D'ORIGINE CONTROLEE

750 ML   ALC.12.5% BY VOLUME

I WAS VERY WELL BROUGHT UP. AS A FIRST PROOF OF SO CAT-egorical a statement, I shall simply say that I was no more than three years old when my father poured out my first full liquer glass of an amber-colored wine which was sent up to him from the Midi, where he was born: the muscat of Frontignan.

The sun breaking from behind clouds, a shock of sensuous pleasure, an illumination of my newborn tastebuds! This initiation ceremony rendered me worthy of wine for all time. A little later I learned to empty my goblet of mulled wine, scented with cinnamon and lemon, as I ate a dinner of boiled chestnuts. At an age when I could still scarcely read, I was spelling out, drop by drop, old light clarets and dazzling Yquems. Champagne appeared in its turn, a murmur of foam, leaping pearls of air providing an accompaniment to birthday and First Communion banquets, complementing the gray truffles from La Puisaye. . . . Good lessons from which I gradu-ated to a familiar and discreet use of wine, not gulped down greedily but measured out into narrow glasses, assimilated mouthful by spaced-out, meditative mouthful.

It was between my eleventh and fifteenth years that this admirable educational program was perfected. My mother was afraid that I was outgrowing my strength and was in danger of a "decline." One by one, she unearthed, from their bed of dry sand, certain bot-tles that had been aging beneath our house in a cellar—which is, thanks be to God, still intact—hewn out of fine, solid granite. I feel envious, when I think back, of the privileged little urchin I was in those days. As an accompaniment to my modest, fill-in meals—a chop, a leg of cold chicken, or one of those hard cheeses, "baked" in the embers of a wood fire and so brittle that one blow of the fist would shatter them into pieces like a pane of glass—I drank Chateau Lafites, Chambertins, and Cortons which had escaped capture by the "Prussians" in 1870. Certain of these wines were already fading, pale, and scented still like a dead rose; they lay on a sediment of tannin that darkened their bottles, but most of them retained their aristocratic ardor and their invigorating powers. The good old days!

I drained that paternal cellar, goblet by goblet, delicately.... My mother would recork the bottle and contemplate the glory of the great French vineyards in my cheeks.

Happy those children who are not made to blow out their stomachs with great glasses of red-tinted water during their meals! Wise those parents who measure out to their progeny a tiny glass of pure wine—and I mean "pure" in the noble sense of the word—and teach them: "Away from the meal table you have the pump, the faucet, the spring, and the filter at your disposal. Water is for quenching the thirst. Wine, according to its quality and the soil where it was grown, is a necessary tonic, a luxury, and a fitting tribute to good food." And is it not also a source of nourishment in itself? Yes, those were the days, when a few true natives of my Burgundy village, gathered around a flagon swathed in dust and spiders' webs, kissing the tips of their fingers from their lips, exclaimed—already—"a nectar!" ♀

PRODUCT OF ARGENTINA

ALC 13.0% BY VOL

TRUMPETER

1997

CHARDONNAY
TUPUNGATO

IT'S TO SHARE

FRANCIS COPPOLA

WE HAD WINE AT THE FAMILY TABLE EVER SINCE I CAN REMEM-
ber. My grandfather had made wine at home all his life. My parents
would water it down, and we didn't really like it. We preferred Coca-
Cola! After my grandfather died, we bought wine in gallon jugs. I
remember that because once, when I was little, I put a pencil through
the loop at the top of the jug to make it easier to carry, and it broke,
and the bottle shattered, and I got in trouble.

As a boy, I liked cold, sweet drinks, as I suppose we all did.
But we did have a drink we called "aquada," which my grandfather
re-fermented from the dregs, with water and sugar added. They'd
drink that until the real wine was ready. I thought that was delicious.

Later on I tried to be sophisticated, but I still wasn't much
of a drinker until I was hired by Bill Cosby to work on a script. He
used to buy Domaine de la Romanée-Conti for his friends. So, at the
age of 22 or 23, I drank a lot of Romanée-Conti at Bill's house. I had
never understood until then that wine could be so delicious.

Wine was certainly connected with memory, of hearing stories of what it was like making it in the basement every year, and giving some to the neighbors; generally an association in my mind with
happiness, sharing, and family. I haven't encountered too many wine
snobs. Perhaps I've been lucky. They're like snobs in any field, with a
need to have their opinions prevail, which is the opposite of people
who genuinely like wine, who tend to be supportive and anxious
really to share. People united by wine see it as the boon it is. ♀

MOSEL - SAAR - RUWER

1959er

Ockfener Bocksteiner feine Auslese

naturrein - Original-Kellerabfüllung

WACHSTUM WEINGUT FORSTMEISTER GELTZ ERBEN
BES.: ZILLIKEN-HARING, SAARBURG-BEURIG BEZ. TRIER

H. D. & CO., T.

BRIDESHEAD REVISITED

EVELYN WAUGH

ONE DAY WE WENT DOWN TO THE CELLARS WITH WILCOX AND saw the empty bays which had once held a vast store of wine; one transept only was used now; there the bins were well stocked, some of them with vintages fifty years old.

"There's been nothing added since his Lordship went abroad," said Wilcox. "A lot of the old wine wants drinking up. We ought to have laid down the eighteens and twenties. I've had several letters about it from the wine merchants, but her Ladyship says to ask Lord Brideshead, and he says to ask his Lordship, and his Lordship says to ask the lawyers. That's how we get low. There's enough here for ten years at the rate it's going, but how shall we be then?"

Wilcox welcomed our interest; we had bottles brought up from every bin, and it was during those tranquil evenings with Sebastian that I first made a serious acquaintance with wine and sowed the seed of that rich harvest which was to be my stay in many barren years. We would sit, he and I, in the Painted Parlour with three bottles open on the table and three glasses before each of us; Sebastian had found a book on winetasting, and we followed its instructions in detail. We warmed the glass slightly at a candle, filled a third of it, swirled the wine round, nursed it in our hands, held it to the light, breathed it, sipped it, filled our mouths with it, and rolled it over the tongue, ringing it on the palate like a coin on a counter, tilted our heads back and let it trickle down our throat.

Then we talked of it and nibbled Bath Oliver biscuits, and passed on to another wine; then back to the first, then on to another, until all three were in circulation and the order of the glasses got confused, and we fell out over which was which, and we passed the glasses to and fro between us until there were six glasses, some of them with mixed wines in them which we had filled from the wrong bottle, till we were obliged to start again with three clean glasses each, and the bottles were empty and our praise of them wilder and more exotic.

" . . . It is a little, shy wine like a gazelle."

"Like a leprechaun."

"Dappled, in a tapestry meadow."

"Like a flute by still water."

" . . . And this is a wise old wine."

"A prophet in a cave."

" . . . And this is a necklace of pearls on a white neck."

"Like a swan."

"Like the last unicorn."

And we would leave the golden candlelight of the dining-room for the starlight outside and sit on the edge of the fountain, cooling our hands in the water and listening drunkenly to its splash and gurgle over the rocks.

"Ought we to be drunk *every* night?" Sebastian asked one morning.

"Yes, I think so."

"I think so too." ♀

PROSPERITY

RED WINE

CALIFORNIA

PRODUCED AND BOTTLED BY
PROSPERITY WINES, LOS OLIVOS, CA.
ALC 13.5% BY VOL

LADIES' HALVES

ELIZABETH DAVID

WHAT ON EARTH COMES OVER WINE WAITERS WHEN THEY TAKE THE orders of a woman entertaining another woman in a restaurant? Twice in one week recently I have dined in different restaurants (not, admittedly, in the expense-account belt of the West End, where women executives have tables and bottles of 1945 Margaux permanently at the ready, or it's nice to think so, anyway) and with different women friends, on one occasion as the hostess and the other as a guest. On both occasions, after the regulation lapse of twenty minutes, the wine waiter brought a half-bottle of the wine ordered instead of a whole one. Please don't think I have anything against half-bottles; on the contrary, I find they have a special charm of their own. There are occasions when a half is what one wants, a half and nothing else, in which case I really don't believe one has to be a master-woman to be capable of specifying one's wishes in the matter. I suppose the assumption on the part of wine waiters that women are too frail to consume or too stingy to pay for a whole bottle must be based on some sort of experience, but instead of having to go back to change the order (ten minutes the second time, one is getting edgy by then, and well into the second course; if they held up the food to synchronize with the wine one mightn't mind so much) he could inquire in the first place, in a discreet way. Or even in an indiscreet way, like the steward on the Edinburgh–London express a few years ago who yelled at me across the rattling crockery and two other bemused passengers, "A bottle, madam? A *whole* bottle? Do you know how large a whole bottle is?" ♀

CHÂTEAU - MARGAUX

GRAND VIN

EN BOUTEILLES AU CHÂTEAU

MIS PREMIER GRAND CRU CLASSÉ

1924

FRANCE

DÉPOSÉ

THE LIFE OF SAMUEL JOHNSON

JAMES BOSWELL

ON WEDNESDAY, APRIL 7, I DINED WITH HIM AT SIR JOSHUA Reynolds'. I have not marked what company was there. Johnson harangued upon the quality of liquors; and spoke with great contempt of claret, as so weak, that "a man would be drowned by it before it made him drunk." He was persuaded to drink one glass of it, that he might judge, not from recollection, which might be dim, but from immediate sensation. He shook his head, and said: "Poor stuff! No, Sir, claret is the liquor for boys; port for men, but he who aspires to be a hero (smiling) must drink brandy. In the first place, the flavor of brandy is most grateful to the palate; and then brandy will do soonest for a man what drinking *can* do for him. There are, indeed, few who are able to drink brandy. That is a power rather to be wished for than attained. And yet, (proceeded he) as in all pleasure hope is a considerable part, I know not but fruition comes too quick by brandy. Florence wine I think the worst; it is wine only to the eye; it is wine neither while you are drinking it, nor after you have drunk it; it neither pleases the taste nor exhilarates the spirit." I reminded him how heartily he and I used to drink wine together, when we were first acquainted; and how I used to have a headache after sitting up with him. He did not like to have this recalled, or, perhaps, thinking that I boasted improperly, resolved to have a witty stroke at me: "Nay, Sir, it was not the *wine* that made your head ache, but the *sense* that I put into it." BOSWELL. "What, Sir! will sense made the head ache?" JOHNSON. "Yes, Sir, (with a smile) when it is not used to it." ♀

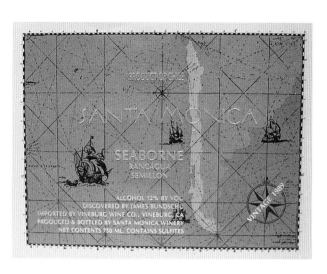

PRODUCT OF CHILE

SANTA MONICA

SEABORNE
RANCAGUA
SEMILLON

ALCOHOL 12% BY VOL.
DISCOVERED BY JAMES BUNDSCHU
IMPORTED BY VINEBURG WINE CO., VINEBURG, CA
PRODUCED & BOTTLED BY SANTA MONICA WINERY
NET CONTENTS 750 ML. CONTAINS SULFITES

VINTAGE 1989

BOOZE

SPALDING GRAY

THE FIRST TIME I SAW WINE WAS WHEN MY UNCLE TINKY brought two bottles of Great Western sparkling burgundy to Gram and Gramp Horton's for Thanksgiving. I sat next to Gram Gray, who didn't like sparkling burgundy all that much, so she took only a few sips and left the rest for me. That meant I had almost two glasses, and that sparkling burgundy made me so happy I wanted more.

I went to my friend Pete, which was short for Meatman Pete, which was an alias for Lowell Prout. Lowell changed his name right after he heard the song "Meatman Pete" on an album called "Songs Your Mother Never Knew." I actually have the album, given to me by the owner of a record store in Warren. The store was right next to a Catholic church, and the owner was afraid of offending the priest who often came in to browse. One day I was in the store looking for the 45 of "WPLJ" (White Port Lemon Juice) by the Four Deuces, and the owner quite suddenly just took the album "Songs Your Mother Never Knew" and said, "Here, do me a favor, get this filth out of here." I grabbed the album and went back to Lowell's to play it. There were some great songs, but the ones I remember best were "Where Can I Find a Cherry for My Banana Split?" and "Meatman Pete." So I went to my friend Pete and said, "Wine is good. Wine is a good thing," and we set out on a quest to find the sparkling burgundy.

We had a plan. We'd drive to the beginning of Mount Hope Bridge, then turn around so we wouldn't have to pay the toll, and head back toward Providence to pick up sailors hitchhiking up to

Newport—older sailors, career men, guys who were over 21 and wouldn't mind buying us booze in exchange for a ride.

When we got to the package store—in Rhode Island they always call liquor stores package stores, I guess because the liquor had to be wrapped in brown paper—we wanted to ask the sailors to buy us sparkling burgundy, but I was too embarrassed. Sparkling burgundy seemed like an unmanly request. So I just told the sailor to get wine, red wine.

He came out with a bottle of Petri port, and that's when Pete and I found out about other kinds of wine. Petri port was sweet ruby red, and had about twice the amount of alcohol as the sparkling burgundy. I missed the bubbles. But it felt thick and warm in my belly as we guzzled it down, late at night, parked in Pete's '49 Ford at the far end of a deserted gravel pit. It made us laugh a lot and feel so good that we wanted more. ♀

MALUMBRES

Crianza 1995

Navarra

Denominación de Origen
Produced and Bottled
by Bodegas
Vicente Malumbres
Corella • Navarra • Spain

MOUNT
VEEDER
WINERY

1996

CABERNET
SAUVIGNON

NAPA VALLEY

ALC. 13.5% BY VOL.

GLOW WINE

LUDWIG BEMELMANS

ON CHRISTMAS EVE, FRAU MAYBOCK WAS DRAINING FAT FROM more geese than she had ever cooked before at one time, while her husband made trip after trip to the cellar to make the Tyrolean Christmas beverage called "glow wine," of which, on that day, every child receives a small glass. It is made as follows for a gathering like the one at the inn: Take four quarts of good dry red wine; add a pound and a half of sugar and an ounce of cinnamon, if possible using cinnamon sticks and breaking them into small pieces. Throw a few cloves into the pot (earthenware if available) and heat to the boiling point. Serve it hot.

It's a good drink to thaw out frozen and lonesome souls, it's a good stopper for colds, it's a quick warmer of the inner man when he comes down from the mountain, and it's the best recipe for the fatigue that follows skiing. ☥

JOSEPH PHELPS

VIN du MISTRAL

CALIFORNIA · 1997

Pastiche

PRODUCED AND BOTTLED BY
JOSEPH PHELPS VINEYARDS
ST. HELENA, CALIFORNIA

A CALIFORNIA
RED TABLE WINE
ALCOHOL 13.5% BY VOLUME

THE WAITER RECOMMENDED THE AUBERGE DE L'ETOILE, AT
Gevrey-Chambertin, a village of blessed associations. At the
Auberge, I fell in with the greatest host of my life—a retired second
lieutenant *de carrière* named Robaine, who had risen from the ranks
in the course of thirty years in the colonial Army. Robaine took me to
all the cellars of the commune and the communes adjoining, repre-
senting me as a rich American bootlegger come to the Côte d'Or, the
Golden Slope of Burgundy, to buy wine for the cargo of a fabulous
bateau-cave—a wine-cellar ship that would be sailed into New York
Harbor and hoisted by night ("like a lifeboat but on a huge scale,
understand?") into a skyscraper with a specially prepared false
front. In that way, I got to drink more good wine than most men are
able to pay for in their lives, and Robaine drank along with me—
"pushing" the merchandise as he drank, and winking grossly at the
proprietors of the vineyards, to indicate that he was conspiring with
them to get a good price from *me*. At night, I would stagger home to
eat the *jambon persillé*—parsley-flavored ham with mustard and
pickles—that every meal began with, followed by hare or beef or fowl
in a sauce of better wine than you could buy in other regions in
labeled bottles. All the good wine I could drink came with the meals,
but Robaine had invented the bootlegger story to get at the superla-
tive wine of the vineyardists. He was a Lorrainer, from Nancy or
Metz, and so an outsider, possessing no vineyards of his own.

One day, I varied the hospitality of the *cavistes* of Gevrey-

Chambertin, Fixin, and Vougeot, the nearest communes, with a pedestrian expedition to Nuits-Saint-Georges, six miles away. There, in the restaurant of one of the two local hotels, I sat at the common table, where I was soon joined by a young man of my own age—a scholarly chap interested in foreigners—who said that he was book-keeper-manager for a local wine merchant. Presently, he asked me how I liked the wine I had before me. The wine was a superb bottle of Grands-Echézeaux, but with a presence of mind learned from Robaine, I said that while it was good, it had limitations. Prodded, I even confessed to a trifle of disappointment. I said I had drunk as good bottles of Burgundy in Paris, even in Ireland; one expected that when one came to the birthplace of wine and asked the proprietress to furnish her best bottle . . . It was one of the most mendacious moments of my life.

The young Frenchman, appalled, said that he would speak to Madame. I begged him not to. He bit his lip. Finally, he said, "I cannot tolerate that you should carry away such a mediocre impression of our cellars. I invite you to sample what we call good wines at *our* place." Looking at the label on my now empty bottle—which was fortunately not that of his firm—he whispered, "Between you and me, the fellow who bottled that, although he is my boss's cousin, is a sharp chap. Doubtful integrity." After that, of course, he had to start me off on something that he considered better than the wine I had downed.

The afternoon I spent in the cellars of his firm was one of the happiest of my life. I regret that I have forgotten the firm's name. I was lucky to remember my own. After sipping the first glass he poured for me, I said, "It certainly beats the other for velvet, but the Echézeaux had a certain vigor, all the same, that is not to be despised." The next, I conceded, had an eternally youthful masculinity—but the Echézeaux, much as I had depreciated it, had had a certain originality. When I had drunk myself as tight as a New Year's Eve balloon, I admitted that the last wine he offered was indeed clearly superior to the bottle at the hotel. This was polite, but a lie. "*That*," I said, "is what I call Burgundy." It was a Romanée-Conti of some sort, and first-rate. "Well worth a voyage from North America to taste. Thunderously superior to that stuff I had with lunch." My benefactor was pale with gratitude. But the bottle at the hotel had been the best of the day.

That short week, thirty-five years ago, was my true initiation into the drinking of Burgundy. ♉

DEVIL'S LAIR

1995

MARGARET RIVER

RED WINE   14% alc./vol.   VIN ROUGE

TAMA JANOWITZ

I WOULDN'T SAY THAT MY FRIEND PAIGE POWELL AND I ARE *serious* wine drinkers, only that we know a decent red wine—and need it—when we drink. We also like to go on adventures, but for some reason every adventure we take leads us to a country where virtually no wine is served.

The first jaunt led us to India. It came as something as a shock to find that wine simply wasn't drunk—let alone made—in Rajasthan. On our horseback expedition, big barrels of Indian beer were served at every break, and at night the expensive stash of vodka and Scotch was proudly displayed. But neither of us are hard liquor consumers, and while I drink beer, Paige despises the stuff. It was only a couple of days before she broke down and—out of thirst and a desire to wash away the dust—started guzzling the lukewarm Kingfisher at 10 in the morning.

At least, we felt, we would be prepared for the next trip: camping and sea kayaking alongside the killer whales in the Johnson Strait of Victoria Island, in Canada's far north. When I met Paige at the airport, her bags were so heavy I couldn't even help her lift them. It turned out that six bottles of red wine were providing the ballast. Unfortunately, the night before we went out we were lectured severely by the guide. "Each of you can bring only what fits into these five tiny waterproof bags," she said. "That's all that can fit in the kayaks."

Paige was all for bringing the bottles along, but I said, "No.

For once in our lives, we're going to travel without too much stuff. Leave them in our locker here at the hotel."

"Oh, all right," Paige agreed. "The brochures did say that alcohol would be served on some nights."

Alas, there wasn't any alcohol served on the first night—and that was when we really needed our favorite Cabernet Sauvignon. We simply weren't cut out for camping, something we had known but tried to block out in the excitement of the prospect of being alongside those orca. We turned out to be the first campers ever to beg to leave the trip after less than 12 hours.

So we rented a car and for the rest of the week roamed the island. Night after night, dining out, we ordered red wine by the glass and the bottle, only to find that all of Victoria Island was accustomed to drinking something that I can only describe as a close relative of Kool-Aid.

We took to carrying an uncorked bottle, secreted in a hand-bag, into the restaurants. Then we would each buy a glass of something undrinkable but nevertheless red. When the waitress was absent, Paige would stroll over to the women's room, glass in hand—or to the bar, when the bartender turned his back. She'd dump out her wine, come back to the table and refill from the pocketbook. Most of the time I forced her to do the same with my glass.

Next we boarded a cruise ship bound for Norway, fore-warned that the liquor there was seriously expensive. Once again the suitcases were laden with Cabernet Sauvignon and Merlot. I was getting accustomed to making a sloshing sound wherever I went. We expected to consume a bottle a night over dinner—that was a half-bottle each—but we weren't expecting that the North Atlantic storms would be such that even we would lose any desire for even a small glass of red. Five days later we staggered off the ship with our supply intact and our suitcases just as heavy as when we began.

I suppose I'm trying to drink my wine and have it too, but while I long for my red wine, I simultaneously long to see places that aren't the same as the place from which I came. Nowadays—when from Tibet to Peru the kids are dressed in the same outfits, get the same American programs via satellite television and communicate internationally via the Internet—the lack of red wine in a particular place may be the only thing left that makes it different.

So until every country in the world stocks the stuff, I'm willing to travel with bottles in my suitcase, weighing down my arms. I can't say I'm getting stronger—but my arms are definitely getting longer. ♈

THE GROWTH OF MARIE-LOUISE

JOHN le CARRÉ

IT HAD A CURIOUS FLAVOR, THAT GREAT WINE, EVEN WHEN IT was new; it is with me still as I write. I knew nothing of wine in the general way; the cult bored me. Neither then nor now could I be relied upon to detect a great year from an indifferent one. But the wine of Étrouille, harvested in 1953 and first enjoyed (prematurely) in 1954, is like the one tune in the memory of a deaf man. It was constructed like the act of love itself. At first taste, it promised and withheld itself; it lay trembling upon the tongue, begging the reassurance of a kindly palate; this granted, it gently opened, responding to the new, internal intimacy, and suddenly the ecstasy was upon you: a strange but brilliant odor filled the nostrils, infused the palate; the liquid swelled and broke upon the senses; and thus, at last, but slowly, it sank little by little into the perfect languor of a protracted afterglow. I did not by any means wholly enjoy it, for we are not always generous to those who stir us from our apathy, or lull us away from our desires; but I could no more forget it than my first conquest in the field of love. They named it *la Cuvée Marie-Louise* after the girl they had all enjoyed; the outside world saw little of it. Only a few bottles, they say, found their way to the tables of the connoisseur; the lion's share remained in Étrouille, and was quickly consumed by greedy natives before it even had time to mature. ♀

GRGICH HILLS

Napa Valley

CHARDONNAY

1993

PRODUCED AND BOTTLED BY GRGICH HILLS CELLAR
RUTHERFORD, CA · ALC. 13.4% BY VOL. · CONTAINS SULFITES

ORVIETO: FAIR LILY OF UMBRIA

GERALD ASHER

TO THOSE WHO GREW UP WITH THEM, ITALIAN WHITE WINES of the old school—blunt and throaty—are as reassuringly familiar as the pungent salami or the fiercely aged pecorino cheese that accompanied them so convincingly. "We know what we like and like what we know" is true even when what we know and like is not necessarily appreciated by everyone else.

Indeed, urban and international taste today is for lighter, fresher, more aromatic white wines. So Italian growers have been sending their sons to enology schools and sprucing up their cellars with better presses, water-cooled stainless-steel tanks, and sterile bottling lines to make their wines that way. In the course of a decade or two, the standards of making white wine in Italy leapt across centuries. In this transformation, a few wines, inevitably, lost more than they gained and are now indistinguishable from all the other brightly anonymous wines served cold by the glass in restaurants from Milan to Osaka. But change, overall, has brought new life to most Italian white wines. Orvieto, a distinctive wine from Umbria, from vineyards about midway between Rome and Florence, is one of those which have recaptured an identity and a market. . . .

On my last day in Orvieto I skipped lunch in favor of a glass of wine and a few slices of prosciutto of wild boar at the Cantina Foresi. I sat at a table in the sun, on the piazza by the Duomo, known since it was completed many centuries ago as the Golden Lily of Cathedrals. Grazia Foresi, the proprietor's wife, set down for me a glass of pale Orvieto Classico. Its enticingly fresh, almost herbal aroma wafted from the glass, and I told her how different it was from the rustic Orvieto I remembered from the past.

Squinting against the sunlight, she hesitated for a moment before asking: "You like the old-style Orvieto?"

In a nostalgic sense, I do. Faults and all. Just as I like reruns of old Anna Magnani movies. So I shrugged and said, "Sometimes."

In half a minute she had replaced the pale wine in front of me with another: it was a rich, burnt gold. She stood there, waiting for me to take my first swallow. I could smell the wine's rasp. It tugged at my memory even before it caught at my throat.

"It's the wine we keep for our local customers, for the old men," she said. "They enjoy their glass of Orvieto in the afternoon. And that's how they like it."

There was nothing to be said. I smiled. ♈

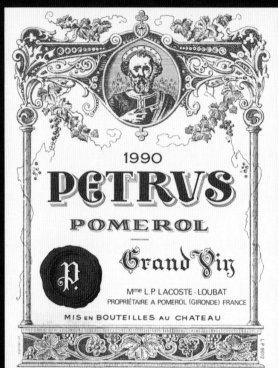

1990

PETRVS

POMEROL

Grand Vin

Mᵐᵉ L.P. LACOSTE · LOUBAT
PROPRIÉTAIRE A POMEROL (GIRONDE) FRANCE

MIS ᴇɴ BOUTEILLES ᴀᴜ CHATEAU

Alc 13,5 % vol   APPELLATION POMEROL CONTRÔLEE   75 cl

TORTILLA FLAT

JOHN STEINBECK

TWO GALLONS IS A GREAT DEAL OF WINE, EVEN FOR TWO paisanos. Spiritually the jugs may be graduated thus: Just below the shoulder of the first bottle, serious and concentrated conversation. Two inches farther down, sweetly sad memory. Three inches more, thoughts of old and satisfactory loves. An inch, thoughts of old and bitter loves. Bottom of the first jug, general and undirected sadness. Shoulder of the second jug, black unholy despondency. Two fingers down, a song of death or longing. A thumb, every other song each one knows. The graduations stop here, for the trail splits and there is no certainty. From this point on anything can happen. ♀

BABETTE'S FEAST

ISAK DINESEN

GENERAL LOEWENHIELM, SOMEWHAT SUSPICIOUS OF HIS WINE, took a sip of it, startled, raised his glass first to his nose and then to his eyes, and sat it down bewildered. "This is very strange!" he thought. "Amontillado! And the finest Amontillado that I have ever tasted." After a moment, in order to test his senses, he took a small spoonful of his soup, took a second spoonful and laid down his spoon. "This is exceedingly strange!" he said to himself. "For surely I am eating turtle-soup—and what turtle-soup!" He was seized by a queer kind of panic and emptied his glass . . .

The boy once more filled the glasses. This time the Brothers and Sisters knew that what they were given to drink was not wine, for it sparkled. It must be some kind of lemonade. The lemonade agreed with their exalted state of mind and seemed to lift them off the ground, into a higher and purer sphere.

General Loewenhielm again set down his glass, turned to his neighbor on the right and said to him: "But surely this is a Veuve Cliquot 1860?" His neighbor looked at him kindly, smiled at him and made a remark about the weather.

Babette's boy had his instructions; he filled the glasses of the Brotherhood only once, but he refilled the General's glass as soon as it was emptied. The General emptied it quickly time after time. For how is a man of sense to behave when he cannot trust his senses? It is better to be drunk than mad.

Most often the people in Berlevaag during the course of a

good meal would come to feel a little heavy. Tonight it was not so. The *convives* grew lighter in weight and lighter of heart the more they ate and drank. They no longer needed to remind themselves of their vow. It was, they realized, when man has not only altogether forgotten but has firmly renounced all ideas of food and drink that he eats and drinks in the right spirit. ♉

COUSIÑO·MACUL

MAIPO

CABERNET SAUVIGNON

ANTIGUAS RESERVAS

RED CHILEAN WINE

BOTTLED BY VIÑA COUSIÑO MACUL · SANTIAGO·CHILE

750 ml   Product of Chile   Alcohol 12% by Volume

LIFE AMONG THE WINESAPS

PETER DE VRIES

"BURGUNDY IS THE KING OF WINES AND CLARET IS THE queen," Almadingen said, bringing a bottle of Médoc to the table in a wicker cradle. I thought how it would be to close my hands around his throat, working the fingers well in under the collar, or to crack him over the scalp with a nice, full-bodied Chambertin. I was not only out of my element but in over my head. I resented particularly the hopelessness of trying to emerge unexposed from the pretense into which I had permitted Almadingen to lure me.

It had been important that we hit it off, because our wives were fond of one another. They were old school friends, and had met again after many years, to find themselves revolving in the same suburban orbit, with husbands who were strangers to each other. When we had all got together for the first time, it had been for dinner at a restaurant in town, and I had been host. "How about some wine?" I had asked, and Almadingen had said, "Capital!" I'd got the idea right away that he was a connoisseur, and to conceal my agitation I had sparred with him across the table, working my lips warily when I sipped and giving him plenty of time to speak first. "This is a tidy Chablis," he'd said, putting his glass down. "Mmm," I had said, nodding assent, thinking that next time it would probably be dinner at the Almadingens' and the strain would be off me.

But would it?

"You should learn to hold your own better when it comes to wines," my wife had said after we'd bade them good night.

"Especially with people like the Almadingens. Look, why don't you read up on the subject?"

During the three weeks before we went to the Almadingens', I had dipped into Grossman's *Guide to Wines, Spirits, and Beers* several times, but had always seemed to get hung up in the chapter on brandies. I'd found a good mot there: "Cognac is like a woman—at her best between the ages of twenty-five and forty," which I intended to use after coffee. I didn't see how I could work it in at dinner, for which we were having a roast of beef and this Médoc of which I have spoken.

"You're a wine man," Almadingen said to me, holding his claret up to the light. "You'll be interested to know that I've been laying in a supply of Bordeaux."

I cleared my throat and held my glass up as Almadingen was holding his, sustaining the pose until I could think of something to say. I said the only thing that came into my head. "Speaking of laying in a supply of Bordeaux," I said, "did you ever hear the one about the hen who laid in a supply of coal?"

My wife dissected her roast beef with cold precision, and Marlis—that's Mrs. Almadingen—emitted a tinkle of mechanical laughter. Almadingen, whose first name is Steve, then went into a reminiscence about how he and several companions had once got into a scrape with the London police while "well in their hock." I never got in the aphorism about brandy. We did have brandy after coffee, but mixed with Bénédictine, and I couldn't very well say "B and B is like a woman," etc. So that washed out.

"I must say *that* was a miserable performance!" my wife

remarked as we rode home in our car. She drove, and I sat slumped down, with my hands in my pockets. "I hope now you'll really brush up. Not that the Almadingens are ever likely to ask us again. Still, we can invite them once more and maybe pull the fat out of the fire. Hens in a supply of coal! Really!"

We asked the Almadingens to dinner at our house a month later, and I crammed for the occasion with a volume entitled *Notes on a Cellar-Book*, by George Saintsbury, as well as with the Grossman. I was reading in the former when I straightened in my chair, plucked by something curiously familiar. "If claret is the queen of natural wines, Burgundy is the king," I read at the head of a section I was beginning. So! I thought: If that's the pitch, O.K.!

Learning well in advance what food my wife planned to serve, I narrowed down my preparations to the three wines indicated. I cribbed some comments and devised some of my own, and when the day rolled around, I was letter-perfect. I even solicited a little co-operation from my wife. "When you hear me speaking of the king and queen of wines," I said, "ask me, 'And the jack?' Sort of casually, you know. Have you got that?"

"I guess so," she said. "But it seems pretty shabby."

"This whole thing is shabby, if you only knew," I said. "Now, have you got that straight?"

The dinner was on a Saturday evening. I drank steadily during cocktails, watching Almadingen as he sat there draining off old-fashioneds with what I thought was an elaborate relish. "You hate his guts," I said to myself. I thought of Almadingen, motionless beside the fire tongs with which I had felled him, down in his cellar laying in a supply of Bordeaux. "Why did you do it?" the police asked. "I was in hock," I said. "I needed some money."

The wines were all white. The first was a dry, moderately chilled bottle to go with the oysters. I sparred with Almadingen again, waiting for him to open his mouth. "Hmm," he said, lowering his glass. "This is a tidy Chablis."

I set my own down.

"This Chablis is impeccable," I said. "Neither the long ocean voyage nor the brutal vehemence of travel by truck seems to have disheveled our sturdy friend. Give me a good white wine. I leave to those who need them the flamboyance of the reds; I'll take this *pierre-à-fusil,* or flinty, taste." I shifted in my chair and went on. "It is as though one, footsore and cloyed by all the blowzy hues of Rubens, Titian, and even Gauguin, came at last, in a gallery, upon the exhilarating understress of the late Piet Mondrian."

Almadingen muttered something and looked into his plate. The women stirred uneasily.

"There are conclusions yet to be attained," I said. "Between the dry, wind-chime tinklings of your Graves and the cloying reverberations of Château d'Yquem—not to detain ourselves with that cracked old cowbell, Riesling—lie the clear peals of Montrachet."

I was dilating in this fashion, each glass building on the stimulation left by its predecessor, when the moment came for which I had planned the latter wine—the arrival of the entrée, roast ham. We finished one bottle and I drew another out of the cooler. They all watched uncomfortably as I set my palm critically against the belly of the bottle, opened it, and poured the wine. "As a lover of wines has put it," I said, bringing my eye momentarily to rest on Almadingen, " 'Burgundy is the king of wines and claret the queen.' Meaning, we know from his context, *red* Burgundy." I paused and waited.

"Is everyone finished?" my wife asked, laying her napkin down on the table. "We can have our dessert and coffee in the living room."

"What, then, is the jack?" I said. Almadingen looked restively from his wife to mine. "It is Montrachet," I said, holding my glass aloft in salute to its contents. The others did not lift theirs but looked fixedly into their plates. "Montrachet, that tawny bastard who has come from a vineyard only eighteen and three-quarter acres in extent"—I paused to drink off half of my glass—"striding robust yet fragrant, muscular but unmistakably perfumed—"

My wife rose, and she and the Almadingens filed into the living room. "Don't you agree this is among the few whites that should be gulped?" I asked, following them and spilling wine from my glass, which I was carrying. Almadingen asked for the bathroom and ran upstairs. "As distinguished from those that should be sipped?" I called to him. I heard the door slam at the head of the stairs.

I had planned to chill a Barsac for dessert, but my wife had slipped out and hidden the bottle in a mess of Cokes under the sink. The means I had used to steel myself for the wine ordeal—heavy drinking—had carried me well into the stage where one is under the impression that everything he says is either penetrating or funny, or both. Almadingen eventually emerged, and as we gathered for dessert, I resumed where I had left off, in a way that I never doubted was hilarious. "It came to me like a theorem," I said, "this division of wines on the basis of how they should be drunk. As a matter of fact, I was in the bathtub when it happened. 'Electrolux!' I cried, as distinguished from 'Eureka!,' and ran naked and dripping through the streets of Westport. 'Wines should be gulped to the extent that they are heavy, sipped to the degree that they are light!' "

The Almadingens' faces were as frozen as the sherbets at which they picked. They left at a quarter after ten.

"Well, you've done it again," my wife said.

"I'll work it out right yet," I said.

"I think you can forget about the Almadingens," she said. "We won't hear from them any more."

Weeks passed—a month—and we didn't hear from the Almadingens. Then, one night, we ran into them at a party. "Go over to Steve and apologize," my wife whispered to me. "He's standing there by himself."

I went up to him. He was leaning against the side of a bookcase with a highball in his hand.

"Say, Steve," I said, "I'm sorry I got so noisy at our place that night. I was just racing my motor. You see, I don't really know about wines. I only know what I like."

He laughed through his nose. "I know damn well what *I* like," he said. He finished off his drink and glanced in the direction of the bar. He seemed flushed.

"You *are* a connoisseur, aren't you?" I asked.

He glared into his empty glass. "I suppose I can tell when

some things are under par," he said. Then he crossed one foot over the other, lounging against the bookcase. "But after the way you ordered in New York that first night, as though you were daring anybody to follow you—" He broke off, and drew himself erect. "I like a glass of wine at dinner, sure," he said. "And even at lunch. But beyond that the demands sometimes made on a man are too—" He stopped, but I followed his glance to the other end of the room, where Marlis stood, watching him. He frowned into his glass again. "This rye has no character, and it certainly has no age," he said.

"That's for sure!" I said. "Maybe I'm particular, because I'm a rye man myself."

He got a fresh drink and came back. "Look, I've got a bottle of fourteen-year-old Overholt I've been looking for somebody to open with—somebody who'll appreciate it. Why don't you drop over some night and we'll get into it?"

"Swell," I said.

We clinked glasses and drank. An hour later, we were linking our voices in old favorites, among them a chorus of "Song of the Vagabonds."

"Sons of France around us, break the chains that bound us, and—to—*hell* with Burgundy!" we sang.

Our wives scowled at us as we went, arm in arm, once more toward the bar. ♈

Sauvignon Blanc Chardonnay Semillon

FiFTh LeG

Margaret River

1998

WHITE WINE-VIN BLANC
PRODUCT OF AUSTRALIA-PRODUIT D'AUSTRALIE

750ml

13.5%
alc./vol.

NOTES ON A CELLAR-BOOK
GEORGE SAINTSBURY

WITH AN UNNAMED HAUT SAUTERNE OF '74, BOTTLED BY ONE of the oldest Edinburgh merchants, but bought at somebody's sale, I have specially fond associations. It was a very rich wine, being about thirty years old when I first had it; in fact, it was too rich for some tastes. But once there came to 'the grey metropolis' a Finnish lady—a most perfect representative of non-Aryan beauty and anythingarian charm—to whom not only all men, but what is more wonderful, most women, fell captive the moment they saw her. She was dining with us once, and confided to me, with a rather piteous *moue*, that, in this country, champagne was 'so dreadfully dry.' Fortunately I had remembered beforehand that the warlocks and witches of the North like sweet things; and had provided a bottle of this very Sauterne, of which I had a few left. She purred over it like one of Freya's own cats (let it be observed that I do *not* think Freya was a Finnish goddess), and I promised her that I would keep the rest for her. But alas! She left Edinburgh in a short time, and after no long one I heard that she was dead. The wine lost half its flavour. ♇

THE COLOSSUS OF MAROUSSI

HENRY MILLER

HE OPENED A BOTTLE OF BLACK WINE, A HEADY, MOLTEN WINE that situated us immediately in the center of the universe with a few olives, some ham, and cheese.... I believe the wine was called *mavrodaphne*. If not it should have been because it is a beautiful black word and describes the wine perfectly. It slips down like molten glass, firing the veins with a heavy red fluid which expands the heart and the mind. One is heavy and light at the same time; one feels as nimble as the antelope and yet powerless to move. The tongue comes unloosed from its mooring, the palate thickens pleasurably, the hands describe thick, loose gestures such as one would love to obtain with a fat, soft pencil. One would like to depict everything in sanguine or Pompeian red with splashes of charcoal and lamp black. Objects become enlarged and blurred, the colors more true and vivid, as they do for the myopic person when he removes his glasses. But above all it makes the heart glow.

I sat and talked with Alexandros in the deaf and dumb language of the heart. In a few minutes I would have to go. I was not unhappy about it; there are experiences so wonderful, so unique, that the thought of prolonging them seems like the basest form of ingratitude. ♀

—1996—

ANDERSON VALLEY, MENDOCINO

Pinot Noir

MÉTHODE À L'ANCIENNE

NAVARRO
Vineyards

ALCOHOL 13.6% BY VOLUME

MIS EN BOUTEILLE AU CHATEAU

CHATEAU COS D'ESTOURNEL

GRAND CRU CLASSÉ EN 1855

SAINT-ESTÈPHE

APPELLATION SAINT-ESTÈPHE CONTROLÉE

1984

SOCIÉTÉ FERMIÈRE DES DOMAINES PRATS A SAINT-ESTÈPHE (GIRONDE) FRANCE

PRODUCE OF FRANCE

THE GRAPES OF RALPH
RALPH STEADMAN

ON OUR WAY TO BORDEAUX, BEFORE WE HAD SEEN HAIR OR hide of a vineyard, we spent the night in Rouen and as always wandered around the town in the early evening engaged in a pleasurable search for something to eat. We chose L'Etoile d'Or, which turned out to be an Algerian restaurant, a really homely place. I chose Algerian wine, La Mouflon d'Or from the Coteaux de Tlemcen, very soft and very round, like sheep's eyes with square pupils. A woolliness too. Then edgy and rocky, steep and sparse, like its name; a mouflon is a mountain goat. The hint of promise got steeper and sparser yet and it began to taste like dull pewter covered in dust and cobwebs stuck to the roof of my mouth. I considered ordering something else, but that was before the couscous and the merguez sausage and brochette arrived. After that the wine held its own and threw itself at my palate like an impetuous ram followed by an avalanche of falling rocks. The magic mix was, of course, the harmony that follows when food and wine from the same region are served together. Apart they taste a little crude. Together they form a delectable symphony of wild and tasty abandon like peasants at play. It made such a modest little place so memorable. ♇

A ROSE FOR WINTER

LAURIE LEE

ON OUR WAY BACK FROM TRIANA, UP THE STREET OF THE Catholic Kings, we looked for a tavern to rest ourselves, and found one called 'Pepito'. It was a lucky chance, for the proprietor was a prodigious epicure, loose-tongued and free-handed. His name was Antonio. He was a bald, youngish man, with a smooth face, shining eyes, stubby ring-covered fingers, and the greasy plumpness that comes from standing long hours behind a bar eating and drinking and waiting for customers. It was his own bar, and he was his own master, and the days were his own to make as pleasant as possible. Seldom, then, did he keep his ringed fingers from picking the food, his fat lips from tasting the many wines of the house. He was an enthusiast, an obsessive, and as soon as we arrived he began to offer us, without charge, glasses of wine from every barrel in the place.

"Approve this," he would say, banging a new one down on the counter and drawing off a little one for himself. Then, as one drank, he would step back a couple of paces, and stand, head on one side, like a painter observing his canvas. "You like it? Solera *buena*. You're right. It's no good. Approve this, then. Oloroso. Very rich. There you are." And bang came another glass, golden as honey, but set down with such force that half of it jumped out on to the floor.

So it went on. For two hours we approved. And for two hours he joined us, glass for glass, sipping holily, watching our eyes while we drank, and telling the history of the wine.

"This is a miracle. Approve the colour. With this you could

suckle a baby. So kind it is. With this you could wash the dead and they'd resurrect themselves. Is stupendous, eh?"

And with every new glass Antonio would bawl to his wife, who was hidden behind a screen, and beg her fry some fresh tit-bit to eat with the wine. Great barrels were piled along the walls, chalked in red with their redolent names: Coñac, Manzanilla, Fino, Tinto, Amontillada, Blanca la Casa, Solera and Especial. We had a glass from each barrel, and from the best, several. If one was not emptied before the next was offered it was tossed airily into the street. And with every glass came some new delicious morsel, cooked by the invisible wife; fried fish, fried birds, kidneys, prawns, chopped pork, octopus, beans and sausage.

Antonio was the fat host of a golden age, persuasive, open-fisted and delighted with our appetites. He cheated himself frivolously for the pleasure of seeing us drink. He talked all the time, and showed us photographs of himself going right back to his mother's breast. And from what we could see the years had hardly changed him at all.

Bewitched by this hospitality, we returned to Antonio another night. We had learned that it was his daughter's birthday, and we brought her cakes. When I placed the parcel on the counter he struck his head with his hand.

"I pollute the house!" he cried, rolling his eyes. "What sympathy, what grace." He bawled to his wife, who immediately began frying. Then he shouted upstairs to his daughter, María, to wash her face and put on fresh ribbons and come down and not dishonour him.

"I pollute the house," he cried again, looking at the cakes in amazement.

His daughter appeared, beautiful and dignified as an *infanta*, and shook our hands. It was her twelfth birthday. She talked to us solemnly about geography and arithmetic, while her father ripped out the corks of special bottles, prised open tins of ham and tunny fish, sent out for cigars, and spread the whole feast before us. And thus we gorged together till after midnight. Antonio was in a frenzy of pleasure, drunk with generosity, riotous and noisy as though at a wedding. María remained cool, courtly, soft spoken and rather prim. But the wife, endlessly frying behind the screen, never appeared at all. ♀

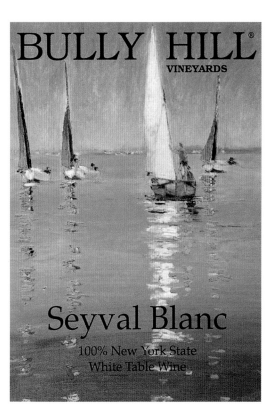

BULLY HILL®
VINEYARDS

Seyval Blanc

100% New York State
White Table Wine

GOURMANDISE

NORMAN MAILER

1.

The wine
　was
　Sierra Blanca
　a California
　　Sauterne.
But it had
　a moldy
　label
and a green
　rusted cork,
age and
　color
　of
　cobweb.
So we
　chose it
over a
　fine dry
　fast
　cool
　professional
　blond
　　from
　Bordeaux.

2.

Yet when

the

nectar

crested

over

the eddies

of fume

which rose

from

the dust

of the cork,

the wine

was sour

and

squalid

like

bad breath

on a good goose

with bad teeth.

Oh, well,

we murmured,

never fall

for a

pretty face

again.

Y

1975

CHATEAU
HAUT-MARBUZET

"Qualité est ma vérité"

APPELLATION
SAINT-ESTÈPHE
CONTROLÉE

H. DUBOSCQ & FILS
PROPRIÉTAIRE A SAINT-ESTÈPHE (GIRONDE)

MIS EN BOUTEILLES
AU CHATEAU

73 cl

LAVENGRO

GEORGE BORROW

I WAS NOW IN THE STRAND, AND, GLANCING ABOUT, I PERceived that I was close by a hotel, which bore over the door the somewhat remarkable name of Holy Lands. Without a moment's hesitation I entered a well-lighted passage, and, turning to the left, I found myself in a well-lighted coffee-room, with a well-dressed and frizzled waiter before me. 'Bring me some claret,' said I, for I was rather faint than hungry, and felt ashamed to give a humbler order to so well-dressed an individual. The waiter looked at me for a moment, then, making a low bow, he bustled off, and I sat myself down in the box nearest to the window. Presently the waiter returned, bearing beneath his left arm a long bottle, and between the fingers of his right hand two large purple glasses; placing the latter on the table, he produced a corkscrew, drew the cork in a twinkling, set the bottle down before me with a bang, and then, standing still, appeared to watch my movements. You think I don't know how to drink a glass of claret, thought I to myself. I'll soon show you how we drink claret where I come from; and, filling one of the glasses to the brim, I flickered it for a moment between my eyes and the lustre, and then held it to my nose; having given that organ full time to test the bouquet of the wine, I applied the glass to my lips, taking a large mouthful of the wine, which I swallowed slowly and by degrees, that the palate might likewise have an opportunity of performing its functions. A second mouthful I disposed of more summarily; then, placing the empty glass on the table, I fixed my eyes on the bottle, and said—

nothing; whereupon the waiter, who had been observing the whole process with considerable attention, made me a bow yet more low than before, and, turning on his heel, retired with a smart chuck of his head, as much as to say It is all right; the young man is used to claret. ♈

MOSEL·SAAR·RUWER

V D P

V D P

FRITZ HAAG

1992

Brauneberger Juffer-Sonnenuhr
Riesling - Spätlese

750 ml   A. P. Nr. 2 577 050 **12** 93   Alc. 8.0 % / Vol.

Qualitätswein mit Prädikat - Erzeugerabfüllung

WEINGUT FRITZ HAAG·DUSEMONDER HOF·D-54472 BRAUNEBERG/MOSEL

WHAT YOU ALWAYS WANTED TO ASK ABOUT WINE
RUSSELL BAKER

MANY READERS HAVE URGED ME TO DIVULGE MY WISDOM about wine, and I do so gladly, for wine is a noble thing, being much slower than the martini (known in bibulous circles as the quick blow to the back of the head) and much harder than differential calculus.

The most common wines are Chablis (rhymes with "wobbly") and Beaujolais (bo-joe-lay). These are excellent wines for beginners because they are easy to pronounce. Neither should be drunk, of course, unless the label bears the words *"appelation controlée"* (meaning "apples under control") and *"mis au domaine,"* which means "put at the domain."

These phrases are the buyer's guarantee that the wine has been made from grapes, with no apples mixed in, and sent to a good domain to acquire breeding, bouquet, good nose, smooth finish, and skill at equitation.

Bottles whose labels bear these phrases are, unfortunately, so expensive that no one can afford to drink them except on a 25th anniversary, and since neither wine will keep for 25 years there is really no point in buying either, especially since, if you are right up on top of a 25th anniversary you would probably rather have three martinis and go to sleep.

Some labels will bear the words *"mis en bouteille dans nos caves,"* which means "bottled in our caves." This wine is made from fermented moss and must always be served at cave temperature. It is the perfect complement to ferns *en brochette.*

In ordering wine at a restaurant, a knowledgeable banter with the wine waiter helps establish one's *savoir-faire*. To avoid humiliation at the outset, the best wine to order is Châteauneuf-du-Pape, since it is relatively easy to pronounce (shot-oh-nuf-dew-pop).

An authoritative question or two creates a forceful impression. "This shot-oh-nuf-dew-pop," you might say, "has it been put at the domain?" or, "Whose caves was it bottled in?"

When the waiter hands you the cork, pass it to your dinner partner and ask him, or her, to squeeze it, then return it to the waiter and ask him to have it chopped very fine and put in the salad. In tasting the wine, roll a small quantity across the palate, then let it settle in the bottom of the mouth and gargle a quantity of air across it and into the lungs, while making loud snoring sounds. Tell the waiter to taste some after objecting that in this particular wine the apples have not been very well controlled.

Having mastered French wines, drinkers will find German wine even more expensive. This is because there is so little of it. The persistent story that Hermann Göring drank it all after the collapse of the Russian front is probably a canard, but it has gone someplace and will not come back for less than $40 or $50 a bottle. It goes beautifully with red cabbage and a Swiss bank account.

For value, the best buys are California and New York wines, but many uninformed sophisticates view them with contempt because they can understand the labels. I have solved this problem with a supply of empty French wine bottles and a funnel. Now my California Cabernet always comes to the table as a *"premier cru"* ("first crew") from Bordeaux.

In the East, unfortunately, the beginner will have to struggle with the wine dealer to get California wine, and this brings us to the crucial subject. Getting one's way at the wine shop.

There are in France huge, underground factories which make a drink compounded of banana skins, random acids, brown sugar and broken shoe strings. Dyed red and bottled, this is shipped to gullible American wine dealers, who sell it as "French country wine."

Merchants with crates of it threatening to eat their way through the cellar floor stalk wine shops on the lookout for innocents, who are always recognizable by the dismay on their faces as they gaze at the price of German wine or wrestle with the distinction between a Côte de Beaune ("Side of bone") and a Côtes du Rhone ("Sides of Rona Barrett").

When the merchant pounces, offering his irresistible bargain in rare French country wine, do not blanch, tremble, yield, or buy. Tell him firmly, "Get me a jug of American wine and a half-dozen French empties." It should come to no more than about $4, and, best of all, it will be made from grapes. ♀

Pfeffingen

1998

Scheurebe

Beerenauslese

JANCIS ROBINSON

TWO WRITER FRIENDS LIVE NEARBY AND WERE ALREADY MAR-
ried in 1970 when I met them. They eat and drink well but wouldn't
dream of buying something as stratospherically priced as Château
d'Yquem for their own consumption. However, when they moved
into a new flat in Hampstead in the early 1970s and found that the
previous owner had left behind a bottle of Yquem 1945, they knew
better than to throw it out. Nor were they unromantic or poor
enough to decide to sell it. Instead they said they'd keep it for a special occasion, the birth of their first child perhaps. They waited, with
great fortitude, more than twenty years, which did the wine no harm,
except that the sweet, sticky wine, kept so carefully on its side,
started leaking through the cork. Alex had apparently asked my
advice on this problem, but must have asked me too late in an
evening for me to appreciate its gravity and I had blithely told him to
keep on storing it horizontally when I should probably have advised
him to recork it, or at the very least stand it up. By the sunny Sunday
evening in July 1994 when about eight of us gathered to celebrate
the conclusion of their agonizingly protracted adoption process, the
bottle was only about four-fifths full. The cork was alive with weevils
or some other form of wildlife and disintegrated as it was extracted.
No food technologist would dream of consuming the liquid beneath
it. No wine lover would dream of doing anything else.

As it turned out, Yquem is such a robust wine that it seemed
completely untroubled by all the air and fungi it had been exposed

to. Some of the others there were no great fans of sweet wine and may well have found it too creamy and syrupy, but I was absolutely knocked out by its richness and concentration. Its trick was that it managed to combine a honey texture with being very much a wine. In fact it was quite intoxicating to sip at this golden relic of the end of the war, while watching the sun set over Hampstead Heath and nibbling the pâté de foie gras I'd brought back specially from Bordeaux (where else?) earlier that week. An ultra-rich experience on all fronts, which we found so agreeable we even broached the 1960 Rabaud Promis, a backup bottle I had guiltily taken along just in case the Yquem had been ruined. This particular event managed to combine all the necessary ingredients for tasting a special bottle: low expectations, some suitably delicious food, no outrageous expenditure, great company, a good excuse, and resultant happiness. ♉

CHALAMBAR

VINTAGE 1992

SHIRAZ

VICTORIA

BOTTLED BY
B. SEPPELT
& SONS LTD.
GREAT WESTERN
AUSTRALIA 3377
PRODUCE OF AUSTRALIA

75CL
12.5% VOL

ALL THAT SHIRAZ!

JAY McINERNEY

"WHAT WILL YOU HAVE TO DRINK?" THE STEWARD ASKED shortly after I had boarded a Quantas jet in Los Angeles, bound for Sydney. It being 11:00 A.M., I requested a Perrier. He raised his eyebrows and frowned at me: "Oh, dear," he said. "You're not going to be much fun." I was reminded of the old Monty Python sketch about the Australian philosophy department, where Rule Number One was "NO NOT DRINKING." (This was also Rule Number Three.) A couple of hours later, when I requested a glass of Aussie Riesling with my lunch, the same steward shook his head. "Not the Riesling," he said. "No?" I asked. "Go with the Sémillon," he insisted. And by God, he was right. At suppertime, just past Hawaii, when I asked for the cabernet, the fastidious steward/sommelier directed me to the Shiraz. If only I had not been so diligent about observing Rule Number One, I might still remember the name of it. Anyway, take my word, it was great.

After a week in Australia—during which I never laid eyes on a vineyard—I concluded that Shiraz is the great Australian grape. And I decided that—besides the cheap wines with which I'd been familiar in the States—the Australians are turning out some spectacular premium wines.

Shiraz (known as Syrah elsewhere) is a warm-weather grape well suited to the temperate zones of southern Australia. Though it may seem absurd to generalize, the typical Australian Shiraz bounds up and introduces itself with a slap on your back, sticks a pot of jam in your nose, then offers to put you up for the night and lend you money. As opposed to the standoffish Rhône Valley Syrah, which usually takes years to open up and address you by your given name. ♈

1996

Viña Rey

Tempranillo

Vinos de Madrid
Denominación de Origen

VINTAGE RESERVE

GUNDLACH
BUNDSCHU

1982
RHINEFARM VINEYARDS
CABERNET SAUVIGNON
SONOMA VALLEY

PRODUCED AND BOTTLED BY
GUNDLACH BUNDSCHU WINERY B.W. 64
VINEBURG, CALIFORNIA 95487
ALCOHOL 13.6% BY VOLUME

REMEMBRANCE OF WINES PAST

HUGH JOHNSON

ONE OF MY GENTLE CORRESPONDENTS WAS MOVED BY BURTON Anderson's article on Lambrusco to express her horror and dismay that we were dignifying in print "the vinous equivalent of rock music."

I am not a great follower of rock music. Nor of Lambrusco. So they certainly have that much in common. But the inference of the letter went much further. It condemned both Lambrusco and rock as beneath critical attention—too popular, too common, too vulgar, in fact, to be any good.

I can't admit this. To give pleasure to huge numbers is itself a virtue. Follow the argument the other way and eventually nothing that pleases more than a few can have any value at all.

I don't like rock, but I do like jazz. From the first creaky acoustic recordings to the smooth bounce of the big bands, it goes, in the words of "Careless Love," "to my head like wine." Which wine in particular is something I have long been trying to figure out. I have tasted first-attempt Chardonnays from California that were like Dizzy Gillespie's solos: all over the place. And the color of his trumpet, too.

On the other hand, a 1977 Sterling Chardonnay recently had the subtle harmonies and lilting vitality of Bix Beiderbecke. Robert Mondavi Reserve Cabernets are Duke Ellington numbers: massed talent in full cry. Benny Goodman is surely a Riesling from Joseph Phelps. Louis Martini's wines have the charm and good manners of Glenn Miller. Joe Heitz, though, is surely Armstrong at the Sunset Café; virtuoso, perverse, and glorious. ♀

THE MARBLE FAUN

NATHANIEL HAWTHORNE

"TOMASO, BRING SOME SUNSHINE!" SAID HE.

The readiest method of obeying this order, one might suppose, would have been to fling wide the green window blinds and let the glow of the summer noon into the carefully shaded room. But, at Monte Beni, with provident caution against the wintry days, when there is little sunshine, and the rainy ones, when there is none, it was the hereditary custom to keep their Sunshine stored away in the cellar. Old Tomaso quickly produced some of it in a small, straw-covered flask, out of which he extracted the cork, and inserted a little cotton wool, to absorb the olive oil that kept the precious liquid from the air.

"This is a wine," observed the Count, "the secret of making which has been kept in our family for centuries upon centuries; nor would it avail any man to steal the secret, unless he could also steal the vineyard, in which alone the Monte Beni grape can be produced. There is little else left me, save that patch of vines. Taste some of their juice, and tell me whether it is worthy to be called Sunshine, for that is its name."

"A glorious name, too!" cried the sculptor.

"Taste it," said Donatello, filling his friend's glass, and pouring likewise a little into his own. "But first smell its fragrance; for the wine is very lavish of it, and will scatter it all abroad."

"Ah, how exquisite!" said Kenyon. "No other wine has a bouquet like this. The flavor must be rare, indeed, if it fulfill the promise of this fragrance, which is like the airy sweetness of youthful hopes, that no realities will ever satisfy!"

This invaluable liquor was of a pale golden hue, like other of the rarest Italian wines, and, if carelessly and irreligiously quaffed, might have been mistaken for a very fine sort of champagne. It was not, however, an effervescing wine, although its delicate piquancy produced a somewhat similar effect upon the palate. Sipping, the guest longed to sip again; but the wine demanded so deliberate a pause, in order to detect the hidden peculiarities and subtle exquisiteness of its flavor, that to drink it was really more a moral than a physical enjoyment. There was a deliciousness in it that eluded analysis, and—like whatever else is superlatively good—was perhaps better appreciated in the memory than by present consciousness.

One of its most ethereal charms lay in the transitory life of the wine's richest qualities; for, while it required a certain leisure and delay, yet if you lingered too long upon the draught, it became disenchanted both of its fragrance and its flavor. ♀

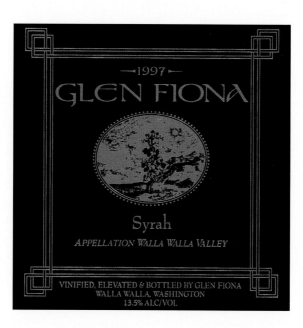

—◄1997►—
GLEN FIONA

Syrah

APPELLATION WALLA WALLA VALLEY

VINIFIED, ELEVATED & BOTTLED BY GLEN FIONA
WALLA WALLA, WASHINGTON
13.5% ALC/VOL

. . . ALMOST AT ONCE DUMAINE SAID, "YOU ARE HUNGRY? THAT'S good. Your menu has been prepared."

Since he seemed to be in a benevolent mood, I asked timidly if I might join him in the kitchen before my lunch. He nodded, and said he would call me. Then he went out back to cut a rump steak for the family's lunch, and his wife volunteered to show me the cellar. She said her husband had walled up one section of it to conceal many bottles of precious wine shortly before the Wehrmacht entered Saulieu, on June 16, 1940. The Germans carried away two truckloads of wine from the hotel, but they never found the cache.

During the war, the hotel was open but the restaurant wasn't, because, much as Dumaine missed his beloved cooking, he didn't want to go in for the black-market buying that would have been necessary to keep operating. But many a Resistance fighter was secretly served a *bifteck* and *pommes frites* by the *grand chef* of the Hôtel de la Côte-d'Or. After the Germans left, the wall was removed, but a number of the fine wines it concealed are still there—all the great vintage years of La Romanée-Conti back to 1926, and an excellent selection of Chambolle-Musigny Les Amoureuses, Charmes-Chambertin, Clos de Vougeot, Romanée St.-Vivant, Volnay Clos des Ducs, Vosne-Romanée Les Grands Suchots, Chambertin Clos de Bèze, and Vosne-Romanée Les Gaudichots.

There is a smaller but still impressive selection of Bordeaux wines; I saw Château d'Yquem '92 and '00, Château Haut-Brion '06,

'28, and '29, Château Cheval-Blanc '24, and Château Ausone '16. Quite a few of the wines in the Dumaine cellar are held in reserve for favorite guests, and not listed on the restaurant's wine card.

"I always try to discourage strangers from ordering one of these irreplaceable bottles," Mme Dumaine said. "The other night, a party of Americans ordered a Romanée-Conti '29, which is listed at 95 francs. One lady put water in it. It was very, very sad, monsieur." ♉

RAVENS

WOOD

ZINFANDEL
ALEXANDER VALLEY
1   9   9   6
VINTED AND BOTTLED BY
R A V E N S W O O D
SONOMA, CALIFORNIA
CONTAINS SULFITES
ALCOHOL 13.8% BY VOL.

MA VIE AVEC LE GRAPE NUT

GAEL GREENE

HOW REFRESHINGLY PRIMITIVE HIS TASTES WERE WHEN WE met. He wanted giant egg creams. No egg, no cream, he explained very patiently, native New Yorker to the aborigine from the Middle West . . . just a dash of milk in the bottom of the cocktail shaker, a big glop of chocolate syrup and seltzer to the top. He wanted orange juice. Fresh squeezed, he said, by my very own left hand pressed against a highly efficient electric juicer, shanghaied from his mother's kitchen. Poor dear. That was her first shattering hint that her precious baby boy might actually Marry That Woman . . . me. Sunning in our penthouse slum, he sipped icy Tuborg beer (he had been until recently engaged to a Danish beauty and an assumed affection for Scandinavian potables had quite naturally developed). When I invited him to dinner he would bring a bottle of whatever the neighborhood liquor store was featuring that week in the $1.19 bin.

Let me say this for the Kultur Maven, longest-running joy of my life, he was always a class guy. Even in those days of blissful solvent poverty. He never even considered the 99-cent specials. He bought $1.19 Chablis and $1.49 Moselle and even Châteauneuf-du-Pape once for $1.99. Even in the glorious green of his innocence, he had an innate sense of where the line falls between *shlock* and *dreck*.

I mean primitive. Refreshingly unmaterialistic. He arrived for the big wedding scene on the lawn in Bloomfield Hills, Michigan, with all his gear in a small canvas gym bag . . . his high school gym bag. What is this wedding twitter? It is a short, predictable story. In the pinch the bride got disgustingly old-fashioned. She put on shoes and got married because she wanted silver that matched and the heirloom Spode. Did I say the groom was primitive? The bride was a simpleton. She'd never heard of the silver auctions at Parke-Bernet.

Never once did I suspect that I had promised to love, honor, and humidify the closet of an incipient oenosnob. They'd never heard of the mythic egg cream in St. Clair, Michigan, where we honeymooned on Lake Huron. But he had hidden a bottle of French champagne in his gym bag. We twirled it in a polyurethane bucket, and, being slightly nervous—living together married after the simple sanity of living together single is fraught with anxiety—we ordered five desserts from room service. The potential for a gourmand future was clear. But I did not suspect he had been bitten by The Grape.

Thinking back, I can see the first signs of serious exposure to oenophilic contamination. I began to cook with early haute pretension. And he stopped heading automatically for the $1.19 wine specials and began consulting the assorted thieves, knaves, and humanitarian wine vendors in our neighborhood liquor shops. We culled some wine lore from the Frenchman next door. Mme. Rochat was an early organic food cultist and the transplanted Rochats never drank anything stronger than papaya tea. But that didn't stifle their natural arrogance on such pitiful American customs as plastic corks and pasteurized wine. (Amazing how the French forget who invented pasteurization.) Then Jules the Ophthalmologist came home from the European fields. It was the peacetime sixties and Jules' war was the Waterloo of his liver in the gastronomic fleshshops in and about the Army hospitals at La Rochelle, France. Jules' budding winesmanship was contagious and appealing. It seemed like a gift, not a disease. When he did his little lecture on the '59 harvest and sang the magic litany of good years and bad years and little fruity vins du pays, crisp but honest whites, humble but charming reds, we sat rapt and envious of such esoteric wisdom.

When my eager mate brought home a '55 Château Margaux to drink with my Swedish meatballs, I had a feeling we were into something over our heads. Our European odyssey with pilgrimages to varied epicurean shrines fueled the obsession. We discovered little nontransportable oenophilic graces like Epomeo, a pale, dry white of Ischia, and Condrieu, the enchanting white wine of the Rhône valley. And there were many pedantic hours spent in oenophilic discourse with other similarly seized souls.

I bought the blossoming oenophile a magnum of 1947 Lafite-Rothschild and a vineyard guide for Christmas. I had to cook a dinner glorious enough to complement the Lafite. It took four days and cost $130. He began to talk about calcareous sand and marl, *Appellation Contrôlée*, premiers grands crus, upper slopes versus lower slopes, racy wines, flabby wines, the mettlesome wines of Lower Burgundy, the fleshy fat Côte de Nuits ... what a cast of characters dominated our lives. He began to practice his oenokultur in the neighborhood, terrorizing a teenage waitress at the pizzeria because she had the innocence to serve Chianti from the refrigerator. She offered to put it through a dishwasher cycle to warm it up ... his scorn was withering. He had amiable waiters in the nearby home-style delicatessen scurrying back and forth to find out the year of a $3 Médoc.

Technique perfected, he took on the pompous *sommeliers* of our town's haughtier French restaurants: sniffing corks, swirling, sniffing, sipping, nibbling, sloshing, chewing, sneering, raising an arrogant eyebrow . . . and, when appropriate, offering a restrained smile of benediction.

He does not speak a word of French. But overnight he graduated from an uncertain "very nice" to a confident "charming," "roguish," "a tannin-wracked little wench," "bien meublé," "puissant," "un peu anémique, non?"

An oenophile's companion must have an unfailing sense of humor. ☿

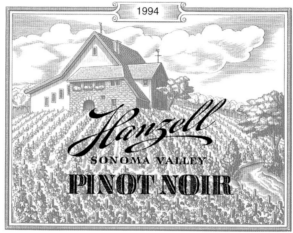

1994

Hanzell

SONOMA VALLEY

PINOT NOIR

Grown and Bottled at the Winery by
HANZELL VINEYARDS, SONOMA, CALIFORNIA

BONDED WINERY #4470 · ALCOHOL 13.7% BY VOLUME · CONTAINS SULFITES

MY LIFE AND LOVES

FRANK HARRIS

MY REPUTATION FOR GIVING GOOD LUNCHES IN LONDON WAS based on the fact that I knew more about the best qualities and the best years of French wines than most people. I have always had a passionate admiration for Rhine wines, too, and the wines of the Moselle. A long time ago now I once earned my living in London by tasting wines: we used to have an excellent lunch, three or four of us, and the six or eight bottles of wine that we had to taste were brought in after we had enjoyed an excellent beefsteak and had cleaned our palates with bread and salt and olives: then each of us had to give his opinion of the various wines and tell especially which would improve with keeping and so be the better purchase. Most of us could give the year of any special vintage. One man in London knew more about white wine even than I did, but I was a good second, and so I may be allowed to speak on French wines at least with some authority.

I remember making every one at the table laugh one day by a comparison between wine and women as the two best things in the world. "Red Bordeaux," I said, is like the lawful wife: an excellent beverage that goes with every dish and enables one to enjoy one's food, and helps one to live.

"But now and then a man wants a change, and champagne is the most complete and exhilarating change from Bordeaux; it is like the woman of the streets: everybody that can afford it tries it sooner or later, but it has no real attraction. It must be taken in moderation: too much of it is apt to give a bad headache, or worse. Like the woman of the streets, it is always within reach and its price is out of all proportion to its worth.

"Moselle is the girl of fourteen to eighteen: light, quick on the tongue with an exquisite, evanescent perfume, but little body; it must be used constantly and in quantities, but must be taken young.

"If you prefer real fragrance or bouquet, you must go to a wine with more body in it, such as Burgundy, Chambertin or Musigny. Burgundy I always think of as the woman of thirty: it has more body than claret, is richer, more generous, with a finer perfume; but it is very intoxicating and should be used with self-restraint.

"Port is the woman of forty: stronger, richer, sweeter than Burgundy; much more body in it but less bouquet; it keeps excellently and ripens with age and can only be drunk freely by youth; in maturity, more than a sip of it is apt to be heavy, and if taken every day is almost certain to give gout. But if you are vigorous and don't fear the consequences, the best wine in the world is crusted Port, half a century old; it is strong with a divine fragrance, heady, intoxicating, but constant use of it is not to be recommended: it affects the health of even its strongest and most passionate admirers and brings them to premature death.

"At their best and worst, wines have curious affinities with women. Young men prefer Burgundy because of its sweetness and fire, while old men always choose Moselle because it is harmless, light, has a delicious perfume and no bad effect." ♀

SAUTERNES-APPELLATION CONTRÔLÉE

Château d'Yquem

Lur-Saluces

· 1947 ·

MIS EN BOUTEILLE AU CHÂTEAU

HOW TO TELL A FINE OLD WINE

JAMES THURBER

IN SPITE OF ALL THAT HAS BEEN WRITTEN ABOUT WINES, THE confusion in the minds of some lay drinkers is just as foggy as it was—in the case of some minds, even foggier. The main trouble, I think, is that the average wine connoisseur has suddenly become rather more the writing man than the sipping man without possessing that fine precision in expository composition which comes only from long years of writing, rewriting, cutting down, and, most especially, throwing away. It is my hope in this article, somehow or other, to clear up a few of the more involved problems of nomenclature and of geographical (or viticultural) distribution, for I believe I know what the wine experts have been trying to say and I believe I can say it perhaps a little more clearly.

France, then, is divided into ninety different *Départements,* all but four of them ending in *"et-Oise"* (and-Oise) and twenty-seven of them having towns named Châlons. Fortunately, in only three of the Châlons *communes* are there *girondes* where any of the great wines of France are grown. We can safely confine ourselves to the Bordeaux region and the Burgundy region, respectively the *Côte-d'Or* and the *Côte de Châlons,* or as the French trainmen say, *"L'autre côté!"* The great wines of France are divided into only three classifications with which we need to be concerned: the *grands vins,* the *petite vin,* and the *vins fins.* And it is with the last that we shall be most particularly concerned. *Vins fins* means, simply enough, "finished wines," that is, wines which did not turn out as well as might have been expected. It is these wines and none others which America is getting today and which America is going to continue to get. Just what causes this I don't exactly know, but something.

In the old days of the great *châteauxiers*, there was never any question about what to do with a vin when it turned out to be *fin*. The *châteauxiers* simply referred to it philosophically as *"fin de siècle"* (finished for good) and threw it out. They would have nothing to do with a wine that wasn't noble, distinguished, dignified, courageous, high-souled, and austere. Nowadays it is different. The *vins fins* are filtered through to the American public in a thousand different disguises, all spurious—not a genuine disguise among them. It is virtually impossible for the layman, when he picks up a bottle labelled "St. Julien-Clos Vougeot-Grandes Veuves, 1465A21, *mise du château*, Perdolio, Premier Cru, Marchanderie: Carton et Cie., 1924," to know whether he is getting, as should be the case with this label, a truly noble St. Estèphe or, as is more likely to be the case, a Benicarló that has been blended with Heaven only knows what, perhaps even a white Margelaise! Well then, how *is* he to know?

Let us say that a bottle has come into our hands labelled as above. "St. Julien" is simply the name of the *commune* and "Clos Vougeot" the name of the chateau around which the grapes are grown. "Grandes Veuves" is either an added distinguishing flourish put on the noble old label years and years ago by some *grandes veuves* (large widows) or it is a meaningless addition placed thereon since repeal by those French *flâneurs* who hope to inveigle the American public into buying cheap and tawdry wines under elaborate and impressive-sounding labels. So much for the name of the wine itself.

The number, 1465A21, is nothing to be bewildered by. It is simply the official *estampe française de la douane* and it can be checked against the authentic "serial-running" of the official French revenue stamping machine by applying to somebody in the French Embassy here, or the French Consulate, and asking him to get in touch with the man in charge of the registered files of the French revenue stamping department. If the letter used (in this case "A") proves to be the actual letter employed in 1924 by the revenue stampers, the vintage date on the bottle is authentic, providing, of course, that the identifying letter was, in that year, inserted between the fourth and fifth figures of the serial number and that 146521 fell among the *estampages* allocated to the St. Julien *commune* in that year. It is, of course, unfortunate that the Stavisky affair in France threw all the numbers in that country into the wildest sort of confusion, so that it is hardly likely that any stamp numbers can be certified with confidence by anybody for the next six months or so. But the wine will be all the better after six months and France may by then have its records in order once more, if she can find them.

The phrase *"mise du château"* is extremely simple, and it is astonishing how many Americans are puzzled by it. It means nothing more than "mice in the chateau," just as it says. The expression goes back to the days, some twenty years ago, when certain French manufacturers of popular "tonic wines" made fortunes almost overnight and in many cases bought up old châteaux, tore them down, and built lavish new ones in the rococo manner. These new chateaux were, of course, clean and well kept, but so garish and ugly that a disdainful expression grew up among the French peasantry in regard to them: *"Ils n'ont jamais de mise du château là-bas"* ("They never have any mice in that chateau over there"). The grand old *châteauxiers* thereupon began to add to their labels, *"mise du château"*—in other words, "There are mice in this chateau," a proud if slightly incongruous legend for a bottle of noble old wine.

The label symbol "Perdolio" on our bottle might equally well have been "Manfreda," "Variola," "Muscatel," "Amontillado," "Sauternes," "Katerina," or any one of a couple of hundred others. The idea of this name originated with the old Spanish *vinteriosos*, especially those of Casanovia and Valencia, and indicated simply a desire on the part of a given merchant to place the name of a favorite daughter, son, mistress, or wine on the bottles he merchandised.

"Premier Cru," which we come to next in looking back at our St. Julien label, means "first growth," that is, wine that was grown first. And "Marchanderie: Carton et Cie." is the name of the shipper. In some cases the name of the captain of the ship transporting the wine is also added to the label, some such name as Graves or Médoc, and one need not take alarm at this, but one should be instantly suspicious of any marks, names, numbers, or symbols other than those I have gone into here. Bottles which bear such legends as "George H., Kansas City, '24" or "C. M. & Bessie B., '18" or "Mrs. P. P. Bliss, Ashtabula, O., '84" or "I Love My Wife But Oh You Kid (1908)" may be put down as having fallen into the hands of American tourists somewhere between the bottling and the shipping. They are doubtlessly refills containing a colored sugar water, if anything at all.

The vintage year is, of course, always branded into the cork of the bottle and is the only kind of bottle-cork date mark to go by. Dates laid in with mother-of-pearl or anything of the sort are simply impressive and invidious attempts to force high prices from the pockets of gullible Americans. So also are French wine labels bearing the American flag or portraits of Washington or such inscriptions, no matter how beautifully engraved or colored, as "Columbia, the Gem of the Ocean" and "When Lilacs Last in the Dooryard Grew."

In summing up, it is perhaps advisable to say a few words about the vineyards themselves. Some vineyards, facing north, get the morning sun just under the right side of the leaf; others, facing south, get the sun on the other side. Many vineyards slope and many others do not. Once in a while one straggles into a graveyard or climbs up on a porch. In each case a difference may or may not be found in the quality of the wine. When a town has been built on the place where a vineyard formerly was, the vineyard is what the French call "out" (a word adopted from our English tennis term). There may be a few vines still producing in gutters and backyards of the town, but the quality of their output will be ignoble. The "out" taste is easily discernible to both the connoisseur and the layman just as is the faint flavor of saddle polish in certain brands of sparkling Burgundy. In the main, it is safe to go by one's taste. Don't let anybody tell you it is one-tenth as hard to tell the taste of a good wine from the taste of a bad wine or even of a so-so wine as some of the *connoisseurs écrivants* would have us believe. ♀

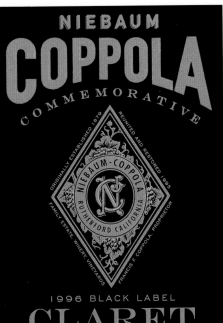

NIEBAUM

COPPOLA

COMMEMORATIVE

ORIGINALLY ESTABLISHED 1879 · REUNITED AND RESTORED 1995

NIEBAUM · COPPOLA

RUTHERFORD CALIFORNIA

FAMILY ESTATE, WINERY, VINEYARDS · FRANCIS F. COPPOLA, PROPRIETOR

1996 BLACK LABEL

CLARET

(MEDOC TYPE)

NORTH COAST

NET CONTENTS 750 ML ♦ ALCOHOL 13.5% BY VOL.

IN PRAISE OF WINE

ALEC WAUGH

AS LONG AS I REMEMBER ANYTHING, I SHALL REMEMBER THOSE two bottles of Château Gris. They will be an amulet against the raucous, self-assertive voices of modernity. Every day life becomes more standardized; more and more do individual idiosyncrasies and eccentricities get ironed out; yet along the slopes that flank the Médoc and the railway line that runs south of Dijon there are these reminders of intrinsic quality, of treasures that have not been casually bestowed; of how in His infinite mercy the great Architect of the universe has set His seal on certain folds of soil. It is a knowledge that restores one's faith in the eternal verities. Whenever the *Mistral* carries me north to Paris and I see those sacred slopes softened by the amber radiance of a Burgundian sunset, I shall remember those two bottles which could have been produced at no other time and in no other place, and I shall see the whole process of living enriched by the miracle that is in wine. ♈

SOCIÉTÉ CIVILE DU DOMAINE DE LA ROMANÉE-CONTI
PROPRIÉTAIRE A VOSNE-ROMANÉE (COTE-D'OR) FRANCE

ROMANÉE-St-VIVANT

MAREY-MONGE

APPELLATION ROMANÉE-St-VIVANT CONTROLÉE

10.105 Bouteilles Récoltées

Nº 001039

LES ASSOCIÉS-GÉRANTS

ANNÉE 1983

Mise en bouteille au domaine
PRODUCT OF FRANCE

75 cl

Excerpt from "Orvieto: Fair Lily of Umbria" from *Vineyard Tales* by Gerald Asher. Copyright © 1996 by Gerald Asher. Published by Chronicle Books, San Francisco. ♆ "What You Always Wanted to Ask About Wine" by Russell Baker. Copyright © 1974 by the New York Times Co. Reprinted by permission. ♆ "Glow Wine" from *La Bonne Table* by Ludwig Bemelmans. Reprinted by permission of David R. Godine, Publisher, Inc. Copyright © 1963 by Madeleine Bemelmans and Barbara Bemelmans as co-executrices of the estate of Ludwig Bemelmans. Reprinted by permission of International Creative Management, Inc., Copyright © Ludwig-es Bemelmans. ♆ Excerpt from *I'll Always Have Paris* by Art Buchwald. Copyright © 1996 by Art Buchwald. Reprinted by permission of the author. ♆ Excerpt from *The Supper of the Lamb* by Robert Farrar Capon. Copyright © 1967, 1969 by Robert Farrar Capon. Reprinted by permission of Farrar, Straus, and Giroux, LLC. ♆ Excerpt from "Wines" from *Earthly Paradise: An Autobiography* by Colette, edited by Robert Phelps. Translation copyright © 1966 and translation copyright renewed © by Farrar, Straus, and Giroux, LLC. Reprinted by permission of Farrar, Straus, and Giroux, LLC, and the Random House Group, Ltd. Published in the U.K. by Secker and Warburg. ♆ "It's to Share" excerpted from interview with Francis Coppola in *Decanter* magazine, December, 1992. Reprinted by permission of Brian St. Pierre. ♆ "Ladies' Halves" excerpted from *An Omelette and a Glass of Wine* by Elizabeth David. Reprinted by permission of The Lyons Press. ♆ "Life Among the Winesaps" by Peter de Vries. Reprinted by permission of the Estate of Peter de Vries. Dever de Vries, executor. ♆ Excerpt from *Babette's Feast* by Isak Dinesen. Copyright 1953, © 1958 by Isak Dinesen. Copyright renewed 1981, 1986 by Isak Dinesen. Reprinted by permission of Random House, Inc. ♆ Excerpt from *As They Were* by M. F. K. Fisher. Copyright © 1982 by M. F. K. Fisher. Reprinted by permission of Alfred A. Knopf, Inc., and Lescher & Lescher, Ltd. ♆ "Booze" excerpted from *Sex and Death to Age 14* by Spalding Gray. Copyright © 1986 by Spalding Gray. Reprinted by permission Vintage Books, a Division of Random House, Inc., and by Macmillan. ♆ "Ma Vie Avec le Grape Nut" from *Bite: A New York Restaurant Strategy for Hedonists, Masochists, Selective Penny Pinchers, and the Upwardly Mobile* by Gael Greene. Copyright © 1971, 1970, 1969, 1968 by Gael Greene. Reprinted with permission of Gael Greene. ♆ Excerpt from *My Life and Loves* by Frank Harris. Copyright © 1925 by Frank Harris. Used by permission of Grove/Atlantic, Inc. ♆

WINE LABEL ACKNOWLEDGMENTS